WWII: LUFTWAFFE COMBAT PLANES & ACES

BY JOE CHRISTY

MODERN AVIATION SERIES

TAB BOOKS

BLUE RIDGE SUMMIT, PA. 17214

FIRST EDITION

FIRST PRINTING

Copyright © 1981 by TAB BOOKS Inc.

Printed in the United States of America

Library of Congress Cataloging in Publication Data

Main entry under title:

WW II : Luftwaffe combat planes & aces.

   "Selected from the extensive files of Wings and Airpower magazines."
   Includes index.
   1. World War, 1939-1945—Aerial operations, German. 2. Germany. Luftwaffe—History—World War, 1939-1945.
I. Christy, Joe.
D787.W18   940.54′4943   80-20998
ISBN 0-8306-9668-7
ISBN 0-8306-2275-6 (pbk.)

The cover of this book features four HA-1112-M1L Spanish aircraft, copies of the BF-109. These aircraft differ from the German originals only in that they are powered by a Rolls-Royce engine similar to that used in the British Spitfire and the American P-51 Mustang. The German BF-109 was powered by an inverted-V Daimler-Benz engine. The photograph is a still from the movie *The Battle of Britain,* in which a dozen or so of these Spanish copies were painted to resemble the almost extinct 109s.

Preface

World War II was truly a global conflict, and the air war—the decisive factor—was differently fought over different parts of the world. Over Europe, the most advanced technologies were employed and the most intense, sustained combat occurred. From the airman's point of view, the Aleutian weather was worse, and the North African deserts or South Pacific islands imposed more primitive living conditions and inadequate diets on aircrews; but over Hitler's *Festung Europa* more airmen died.

Total Luftwaffe combat losses were near 80,000 killed or missing and 30,000 wounded (1945 Luftwaffe records are incomplete). That compares with American and British aircrew losses of 79,265 and 79,281 respectively, killed or missing for the entire war.

Russian air losses are unavailable to Western researchers, but Luftwaffe records show 45,000 Soviet planes destroyed, for a loss of 4,948 German aircraft destroyed or "more than 10% damaged." That is a kill/loss ratio of nearly ten-to-one. The Soviets, with their usual disregard for the truth, claimed 60,000 German aircraft destroyed. The Germans, on the other hand, list 35,000 British and American planes destroyed during 68 months of combat, a remarkably accurate figure.

German aircraft production, 1939-1945 inclusive, totalled 113,514, including 86,310 combat airplanes. Since the U.S. and British claimed 57,000 German airplanes destroyed in combat and on the ground, total Luftwaffe plane losses in combat would be 61,900 counting those destroyed in Russia, and suggests that an additional 25,000 German combat planes were lost to battle damage but not counted by the Allies, to accidents, and to capture at war's end.

Germany, of course, had no strategic bomber force in WWII. The Luftwaffe was essentially fitted for close air support of the German ground forces and the *Blitzkrieg*, or "Lightning War" concept—and, as events later demanded, defense of the Reich against Allied bombing attacks.

While the Luftwaffe was primarily structured to spearhead *Panzer* attacks for the conquest of Europe, Luftwaffe leaders clearly understood that effective support of the mobile ground units depended upon control of the air. Luftwaffe Chief of Staff Lt/Gen Hans Jeschonnek was a disciple of Italy's great air strategist, Gen Giulio Douhet, who had, as early as 1921, in his book *Air Power*, set forth the basic principles of air warfare in the following order: 1. Destruction of the enemy air force, 2. close air support of advancing ground forces, and 3. attack the enemy's sources of strength; i.e. the centers of war industry, communications, and transport.

The Luftwaffe followed these precepts during the invasion of Poland, which began WWII on September 1, 1939, and with only slight deviations retained this order of precedence throughout the war, or as long as it was able to do so.

After the United States was forced into the war, both President Roosevelt and Prime Minister Churchill agreed that defeat of Germany (and Italy) should be given priority over the war with Japan, and the major U.S. effort was directed to that end, beginning with the invasion of North Africa in November, 1942.

The Allied drive from North Africa through Italy spread the Luftwaffe very thin indeed at a time when fierce fighting continued on the Russian Front and the U.S. strategic bombing of Germany was building from still another direction.

The coordinated strategic air offensive against Germany began early in 1944, and by early March 1,000 American heavy bombers per raid were devastating Berlin. By the end of March the Luftwaffe had lost more than 800 fighters in air battles with U.S. bombers and fighters. This, coupled with nightly Royal Air Force strikes of fantastic bomb-tonnage, and low-level attacks on German airfields by American medium bombers, achieved Allied air superiority over Europe by April of 1944. From that time on, every air commander on both sides knew that Hitler's Third Reich was doomed.

Joe Christy

Contents

Acknowledgments

Portions of this material first appeared in *Wings* and *Airpower* magazines.

The introductory material in Chapter 5 is excerpted from *The German Air Force Versus Russia, 1941* by Generalleutnant Hermann Plocher. It is one of ten books in the series The German Air Force in World War II written by key Luftwaffe officers for the USAF Historical Studies series.

The assistance of Dr. Kurt Tank and Oskar Romm is appreciated in providing information in Chapter 8.

Photographs are courtesy of: NASM, William Green, Air Force Museum, Dornier via James Crow, H. J. Nowarra, Imperial War Museum, E. C. Armees France, USAF, Franz Stigler, Archiv Redemann, John Caler, Bildarchiv (Georg Fischbach), National Archives, Rudolf Opitz, Flight, and Peter M. Bowers.

Chapter 1
The Stuka

Note: Dive bombing was developed in the United States and it was there, during the years between the wars, that its techniques were exploited to the fullest, particularly by the U.S. Navy. Nevertheless, by the mid 1930s, single engined dive bombers had given way to twin engined attack aircraft and by the outbreak of WW II, the United States which has pioneered this unique engine of war, no longer had a significant inventory of dive bombers in its Air Corps.

True, the Navy retained the incomparable Douglas SBD Dauntless, an aircraft designed in the mid 30s, but new dive bombers never fully succeeded in carrying on the tradition pioneered by the carrier strike squadrons of *Lexington* and *Saratoga*. The Curtiss SB2C Helldiver was painfully slow in demelopment and late into combat, appearing in strength only after the major carrier battles in the Pacific had been fought. Meanwhile, in the Air Corps, no new dive bombing aircraft succeeded the SBD's first cousin, the Northrop A-17, and although the emerging P-51 fighter was produced briefly as the A-36 attack plane its promise was only fully realized in the pure fighter role and its dive bomber series was abandoned.

What would have happened had the Air Corps continued to build single engined dive bombers is now a matter of conjecture, but if it had, our own A-17 may well have been the Ju 87 Stuka of America with the same disappointing results. For the A-17 and the German dive bomber were direct contemporaries, conceived and tested during the same period. The former was abandoned, and rightly so, as being obsolete and inferior to the new, swift attack aircraft such as the A-20 Havoc, but the latter was kept in production, long after it had outlived its usefulness. Its subsequent career, after the lightning successes of the first full year of war, only serves to reinforce the decision of those American war planners who chose to cast their lot with twin-engined attack aircraft.

Nevertheless, for nearly a year, in the skies over Poland and France, the name Stuka, conjured up the frightful epitome of Adolf Hitler's lightning War. □

The Ju 87 Stuka, an abbreviation for the German **Sturzkampfflugzeug**, or simply strike aircraft, was adopted by the newly emerging Luftwaffe on the strength of two men's recommendations and the work of two engineers (Fig. 1-1). The first, Ernst Udet, a former WW I German fighter ace and a combination of Billy Mitchell, Jimmy Doolittle and Roscoe Turner, had visited the United States frequently during the 30s, appearing at air races and fly-ins. He was a habitual guest of the U.S. Navy and, although without official position, recommended to his former comrade in arms, Herman Goering, then head of the Luftwaffe, that the new German air force adopt the dive bombing methods and aircraft of the U.S. Navy.

Udet had seen practice demonstrations of dive bombing by the pilots of Bombing Five and Three, and he not only praised the skill of the navy's carrier squadrons, but urged Goering to procure similar aircraft (Curtiss BFC and BF2C Hawks) in order to carry on further tests in Germany. Unfortunately, the head of technical procurement for the Luftwaffe, Wolfram von Richthofen, had no faith in dive bombers and although the Germans had developed a dive bomber some years before, at their Junkers subsidiary in Sweden, additional testing had not been encourgaed and the project had been allowed to lapse. However, upon Udet's repeated testimony and with Goering as chief of a revitalized Luftwaffe, which had the full support and backing of the Fuhrer, the dive bombing project was revived. Richthofen was sent to Spain and Udet was made head of the Luftwaffe's technical branch.

Given a free hand, contracts were quickly let to improve upon what Udet had seen in the United States. Two Curtiss Hawks were purchased for testing and Focke-Wulf Fw 56 fighter trainer biplanes were also fitted with bomb racks to provide additional test machines. Among those firms given an order for one prototype was Junkers and its project designer, Herman Pholmann, quickly recalled the earlier dive bomber he and Karl Plauth had worked on while in Sweden. Plauth had since died in a crash, but Pohlmann had enough test data to reconfigure the old Junkers K-47 airframe into the mockup of what was to become the Ju 87 (Fig. 1-2).

Early Prototype

Both had been low-wing, two-seater monoplanes, but the Ju 87 prototype featured, among other innovations, a closed canopy, a landing gear enclosed in enormous fairings and inverted gullwings, to reduce the length of the gear and yet provide room for a 1000 lb.

Fig. 1-1. Its pointed spinner and grinning radiator intake, its heavily spatted gear thrust down like the claws of a bird of prey, the Ju 87 Stuka embodied the spirit of blitzkrieg warfare. An air-driven siren on its right landing gear was calculated to infuse terror during its dive bombing attacks.

bomb. However, the small twin ruddered empennage of the K-47 was retained.

Service tests soon showed that the Ju 87's main competition would come from the modern Heinkel 118, a much faster craft, but Junkers had a great deal of influence within the air ministry and when Udet, still not ready to accept the defeat of the He 118 prototype, crashed while flying it, the selection of the Ju 87 was assured (Fig. 1-3).

In actual fact, the Ju 87 had proven itself the sturdiest of the competitors, but it was already June, 1936 and it did not augur well for the Luftwaffe that its dive bomber, already obsolescent in both looks and performance, was still in its prototype stage.

While Udet had been correct in his assumption that dive bombers ranging ahead of the German land armies would be able to act as flying artillery, pulverizing enemy strongpoints and destroying communication and transportation networks immediately behind the front lines, he had chosen the wrong weapon to carry out his thesis. Even during the last days of 1937 when the Stuka was first sent to Spain (Fig. 1-4), it could not be considered a modern strike aircraft. Two years later, over Poland, it would be obsolete.

Yet the Ju 87 achieved its greatest success over Poland in 1939 and in France the following year.

The truth of this statement would seem to belie the report that the Stuka was already over the hill in the late 30s (Fig. 1-5). In fact,

Fig. 1-2. The final pre-production test model of the Stuka was the Ju 87 V-4. The engine had been lowered, the distinctive angular tail added and tested in the V-2 and V-3 versions.

the success of the Junkers dive bomber in 1939 and 1940, forced Luftwaffe procurement officials to close their eyes to the truth and keep the Ju 87 in production as late as 1944, when 1,012 of them were completed, the Stuka's second most productive year on the assembly lines.

Incredibly Slow

In order to understand the reasons for the Ju 87's success during the early part of the war, one must be aware of the considerable handicaps it took into battle with it. First and foremost, it was incredibly slow, under 200 mph. in the B model, with a full bomb load (Fig. 1-6). Range with this 1,000 lb. load was only 370 miles. Its protective armament was puny, consisting of three rifle caliber machine guns, and although it was a sturdy machine, it was not maneuverable (Figs. 1-7 and 1-8). Its landing speed of 75 mph. while not particularly high, was similar to an SBD, but the SBD could carry its 1,000 lb. payload nearly 1,000 miles and do it at speeds over 200 mph. As for maneuverability, the SBD was one bomber which handled like a fighter, the Ju 87 was awkward and unresponsive.

Captain James MacDonald who flew with the U.S. Air Force over Africa in the winter of 1942-43, recalls jumping a flight of six Ju-87D Stukas over El Guetar. Before they knew it, I was among them. They were so slow and ungainly, that it was more like shooting at defenseless targets than war. I blew up four within two

Fig. 1-3. The original Stuka V-1 with Rolls Royce Kestrel engine. The famed Rolls Royce Merlin engine evolved from the Kestrel. This airplane was destroyed when its twin rudders developed flutter in a test dive.

or three minutes. They couldn't run. They couldn't maneuver. They couldn't fight back. I would have gotten them all, if my ammunition had lasted." Captain MacDonald's aircraft was a Spitfire Mk. IX and half his ammunition had been already expended against an escorting Me 109, which he also shot down. For this action he received the DFC.

The fact that the Stuka could not survive any sort of determined fighter attack was ignored by the Luftwaffe, simply because

Fig. 1-4. Early model Stukas were sent to Spain late in 1937 to fight in the Spanish Civil War with the Luftwaffe's Condor Legion. By the time Hitler invaded Poland, in September, 1939 to start WW-II, the Stuka was obsolescent, but it was to remain in service and to fight on all European fronts, in Russia and North Africa.

11

Fig. 1-5. The 12th production Ju 87A-1. Powered with a 635-hp Jumo engine, and armed with only two rifle-caliber machine guns, this version equipped a number of Luftwaffe dive bomber Gruppen during the first year of the war. Horsepower doubled in later models.

in Spain and over Poland and France, such opposition never materialized. By the time the first Ju 87 A-1s began their regular bombing runs on the Spanish ports of Valencia, Barcelona and Tarragona, in the latter half of 1938, the Republicans had little to resist them with. Therefore the fact that this first model could not even break 200 mph. (even without a bomb load) and that in order to carry even 500 lb. of bombs, the rear guner had to be deleted, was not of critical import. Nevertheless it must have disturbed Luftwaffe planners to contemplate what might happen to their new dive bomber, if it should come up against an enemy capable of inflicting damage.

The need to answer this vexing problem did not arise until the summer of 1940. By then the Stuka had blitzed Poland and shattered the French. Ranging far ahead of the Wehrmacht's panzer thrusts, virtually unopposed dive bombing strongpoints and pockets of stubborn resistance out of existence became little more than perfunctory exercise. The missions might be a bit more realistic than battle practice, but with the Polish Air Force destroyed in three days and the French unable to send up fighters for days at a time, they were executed with an almost perfunctory discipline. A trail of smashed defenses below' broken truck columns, and hordes of stragglers huddling in ditches were the stuff that propaganda was made of. The howling Stuka was invincible. The awkward, ugly bird merely had to dive—the wind driven siren on its starboard wheelpant, adding to the din of crashing bombs and rushing air, thoroughly demoralizing all who heard it—and victory was assured.

The Ultimate Weapon

For some months the world believed this. Both the Germans and their enemies believed it. Even the neutrals believed it. The Stuka was the ultimate weapon. Then the raids on English shipping in the Channel, preparatory to Hitler's invasion, and the unbeatable Stuka was no more. Against tough fighter opposition put up by the RAF, Stuka losses with or without fighter escort, were murderous and on August 13, 1940, the Stuka strength of Flying Corps VIII was cut by nearly one fourth of its original 220 machines. From that time on the Stuka would play a stop-gap role in all forthcoming operations. Newer, improved models would be built. They would be converted to tank-busters, night attack bomber, strike aircraft against Balkan countries without air forces to defend them, or they would be given to less fortunate Allies. But despite these new assignments, the Luftwaffe's continued use of the Stuka was dictated more by the fact that production lines to turn them out were already running (and could not be shut down for some time and reconfigured to turn out other aircraft) than any great satisfaction with the Stuka's performance. Easy successes rather than operational promise had dictated production of the Junkers Ju 87 and in its third year of war, the hardpressed Luftwaffe would be forced to utilize it.

Fig. 1-6. Flaps and dive brakes down, a Ju 87B-2 comes in for a landing at an Italian air base. Slow and not particularly maneuverable, the Stuka was stable and would absorb a great deal of punishment. These craft had no bombsight as such, but used a series of red lines painted on the cockpit's side panels which were lined-up with the horizon to obtain the proper dive angle.

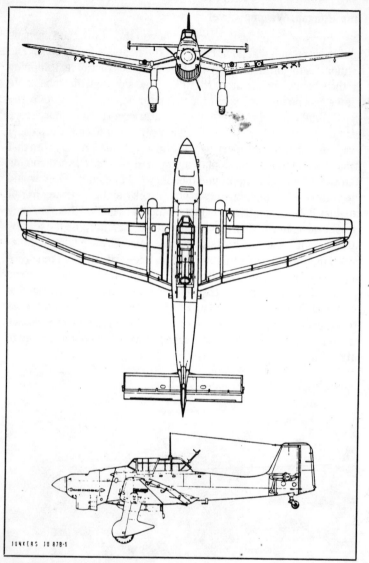

Fig. 1-7. Junkers Ju 87B-1 Stuka three-view.

Bigger engines, which more than doubled the horsepower of the original prototype helped somewhat and the Stuka was able to carry a more respectable bomb load, but its maximum speed, clean, without bombs, never topped 255 mph. With any load over half a ton, speed was still 200 mph. And despite the added horsepower, the airframe never a revolutionary one or particularly inspired, could not be stretched to increase performance. To somewhat offset its defensive liabilities and lack of speed, it was used as a night bomber, particularly in the East, and it was also on the Russian front that the Stuka played out its most important role since the opening months of blitzkrieg.

The Russian Front

The war in the East was unique, in that virtually all aerial missions were tired to the ground armies. Strategic airpower was virtually an academic proposition, and because the course of the land fighting hinged on the performance of tanks, that vehicle was as important on the Russian steppe as it had been on the wastes of the Libyan desert. The Wehrmacht's key function was to contain the excellent Russian tanks. It did not have enough of its own tanks and anti-tank guns to do so, thus it had to rely on airpower to provide the remaining force.

Unfortunately, for the supply and technical arm of the Luftwaffe, there wasn't enough tactical airpower available for the job. The Henschel 129, was one of the few aircraft the Germans had, built especially for a tactical anti-tank role. The Junkers Ju-88 fighter bomber was also pressed into service, and, by virtue of the fact that it was a superlative flying machine, it contributed greatly to the blunting of Russian tank spearheads. These measures not-

Fig. 1-8. The Stuka Ju 87B-1 had a maximum speed of 217 mph at 16,400 ft; maximum dive speed of 373 mph, and carried one 1,100-lb bomb beneath the fuselage along with one 110-lb bomb under each wing. Normal armament was a pair of 7.9-mm machine guns in each wing and a single gun on a flex mount in the rear cockpit.

withstanding, the lack of tactical aircraft and anti-tank aircraft in particular, remained a sorepoint. As a result, the Ju-87D was converted into a tank-buster (Fig. 1-9).

Actually, the later G models were merely modified Ds, with different offensive firepower. In addition to this armament which was eventually increased from 20mm to 37 mm cannon, slung under the wings, the reconfigured Stukas were laden with more and more armor plate. With so much armament, armor and bombs hung on the aircraft, the Stuka became an unwieldy bird to fly. It struggled, rather than flew through the air and standard operating procedure was to first drop the crutchheld bomb from below the fuselage, in order to lighten the aircraft and improve its flying characteristics, and then attack with cannon (Fig. 1-10).

This tactic worked in Russia, until the Red Air Force's fighter defenses improved. By 1943, it took a Major Rudel or a Captain Zemsky to destory Russian armor, elude Russian fighters and still return to base. Few Stuka crews were able to emulate them, although the amazing Rudel was credited with an almost unbelievable 2500 combat missions, which averages out to almost two a day for four years of war. In that time, Rudel destroyed 500 tanks, innumerable trucks and soft transport, as well as the Russian battleship *Marat*.

Fig. 1-9. The Stuka's last role was that of tank-buster, in which it was employed almost exclusively on the Russian Front. Dive brakes were removed and two 37-mm cannons were installed in pods beneath the wings. This degraded aircraft performance, but the Stuka was effective in Russia and, to a somewhat lesser extent in North Africa.

Fig. 1-10. Mottled finish was applied with water-based paint for winter operations in Russia.

Despite the efforts of pilots like Rudel, the Stuka could no longer function adequately in modern war. Armored head shielding, back plates and side plates in the cockpit, did little to deflect the heavier caliber machine gun bullets and cannon shells. The rear gunner's twin .30 caliber defensive machine guns, offered little protection to the aircraft. Its forward firing guns were good only for strafing and it was now so ham-fisted a machine, that even elementary evasive maneuvers were no longer available to its pilots. By the end of 1943, the Stuka was cold meat.

When fully loaded for tank-hunting it could not break 200 mph. Its rate of climb was one-fifth that of the slowest Russian fighter. At low altitudes, it was dangerous to fly. Never maneuverable, it was no aircraft to hedgehop in and its maximum ceiling of 24,000 ft. ruled out escape by that route. Employed in line abreast waves, against tanks which advanced over the ground in a similar formation, the Stukas often succeeded in blunting armored thrusts by bombing and through the fire of their heavy anti-tank cannon. But after their initial strike, they were usually decimated by enemy fighters, particularly during the last two years of the war, when the Luftwaffe could no longer provide adequate air cover.

In all, a total of 4881 Stukas were completed. Of these 2,684 were the improved D and G models, the remainder being the classic B-1 and 2. Although it was hopelessly outclassed by 1943, 1,672 Ju 87s were completed, while a further, 1,012 were delivered in 1944, when production ceased.

Karl Toll

Chapter 2
The HS 129 Flying Can Opener

Sworn by—by few—sworn at—by many, the Luftwaffe's Henschel Hs 129 tank destroyer never quite fulfilled the performance promise for which it had been designed. A controversial subject throughout its development and operational career, thirty years later the Hs 129 still divides aviation enthusiasts on its relative shortcomings and merits.

In early 1937, while the thoughts of war were still far from the minds of the majority of the world's people, the military planners in the *Reichluftfarhrtministerium* (RLM), or German Air Ministry, were laying the foundation for the procurement by the Luftwaffe of a *Schlachtflugzeug* (close support aircraft). With the improved armor plating and performance already developed by both Germany and her future enemies, in the production of advanced tanks and mobile firepower, the Air Ministry fully realized the inadequacies of the then available close support anti-tank aircraft, the Heinkel 51 biplane with its six 22 lb. bombs, as well as the newer JU 87 *Stuka*, which had yet to make its debut over Spain. The need for a fast, maneuverable, heavily armored, and well armed close support and attack aircraft was evident. Even more obvious was the need to design an aircraft built expressly for the ground support mission.

With this in mind, the Air Ministry issued a preliminary design specification to the German aircraft industry, in April 1937, for such a plane. Among the companies which received this request were Gotha, Henschel, and Focke-Wulf. The Air Ministry requirements called for a twin-engined, fixed-forward-firing cannon-platform, that would present as small a target or silhouette as possible. The aircraft also would include a high degree of pilot protection through the use of a heavily armored cockpit and windshield area. The Ministry received the industry proposals in the Fall of 1937 and after much comparison and feasibility evaluation of the various concepts, awarded parallel contracts to both Focke-Wulf and Henschel for design and development. For the following two years the companies competed for the prototype award through numerous mock-up inspections, design modifications, and preliminary flight trials.

Focke-Wulf, under the leadership of Kurt Tank (famous designer of the FW 190 fighter) proposed to modify its already designed FW 189 *"Eule"* (Owl) twin-boomed reconnaissance aircraft for the close support role. Its basic design was altered by adding heavy armor plating around the previously glass enclosed crew compartment, and by the installation of two-20mm cannons and four 7.9 mm MG 17 machine guns between the crew compartment and the engine nacelles. Designated the FW 189V6, only one prototype of this aircraft was completed before the Air Ministry contract was awarded to the Henschel design.

The first three Henschel prototypes were given the typical V designations: Hs 129V-1, V-2 and V-3, and by the summer of 1939 were progressing through a flight test evaluation program. Powered by two Argus As 410A-1 465 hp air-cooled inline engines, the single-seat Hs 129 prototype was armed with two 20 mm MGFF cannons and two 7.9 mm MG 17 machine guns mounted on each side of the armored cockpit and aimed through a Revi C12/C gunsight positioned just forward of the windshield on the fuselage nose section.

Underpowered

The debut of the new ground attack ship was not a propitious one. It was underpowered, clumsy on the controls, sluggish, slow, unable to maneuver to even minimum standards and, worst of all, jammed into a tiny coffin-like cockpit, its pilots were practically blind. All this notwithstanding, the go-ahead was given to Henschel to proceed with the fabrication of eight pre-production models, designated Hs 129A-0, which were assigned to the 5th *Staffel* (approximately 12 aircraft) of *Lehrgeschwader* 2 (operational training wing) for final test and flight evaluation. Much to the dismay of Henschel, the opinions of the Luftwaffe test pilots were generally unfavorable. They stated in their reports that the new plane was still underpowered, was difficult to handle on simple formation maneuvers with very slow response to control actuation, and that its forward visibility through the heavily armored enclosed cockpit with its slit-like clear areas, was almost non-existent. Based on these reports, the Ministry requested that Henschel halt fabrication and investigate ways to modify and improve the aircraft (at the same time the Ministry assigned the remaining Hs 129A-0s to a Luftwaffe training unit in Paris). Among recommendations for improvements were an airframe change to accept the French Gnome-Rhone 14M 700 hp radial engine (which had powered the French Breguet 690 series attack bomber, before the fall of France), and an increase in forward visibility through redesign of the cockpit layout and windshield area. These modifications were made by Henschel with surprising ease, although the first redesign with the French engines, provided even worse vision than the original. However extensive rework corrected the problem and an order was placed by the Air Ministry for ten Hs 129B-0 models, the first of which was delivered to the Luftwaffe at the end of 1941. The improved flight characteristics and visibility of this model due to a reduction in stick forces through the use of electrically actuated trim tabs on control surfaces and the incorporation of larger windows all around, were enough to convince the Air Ministry of the feasibility of the plane, and orders were placed for the first production version which was designated the Hs 129B-1. However weight had risen markedly and this problem was to plague the 129 throughout its career, as more and heavier armament and defensive armor plate were added (Fig. 2-1).

Assigned to the 4th *Staffel* or *Schlachtgeschwader* 1(4/Sch. G.1) which had been formed in early 1942 at Lippstadt, these aircraft, formed specifically as a close support and ground attack unit, were posted to the Eastern Front in May 1942 for their first combat encounter against Russian armor.

Engine Problems

In Russia, immediate problems with the Gnome-Rhone radial power-plants became apparent. They were found to possess poor reliability and serviceability, were chronically susceptible to dust, and could not sustain any measure of combat damage without complete loss of power. Again, production was halted by the Air Ministry in a frantic effort to solve the engine problems. Although never completely eliminated, the difficulties were, to some degree, reduced in severity, and based on these results production was resumed. In addition, the Luftwaffe formed two more Hs 129 units in September 1942. The first, the 4th *Staffel* of Sch.G.2 (4/Sch.G.2) was organized in Poland, and the second, the *Panzer*

Fig. 2-1. This Henschel Hs 129B displays "FE" numbers on tail and beneath wings indicating it was a captured enemy aircraft in the possession of the USAAF at the end of WW-II. American engineers closely examining the craft were surprised to find that it contained so much armor that it weighed almost four and a-half tons empty. Its length was but 32 ft.

Jager Staffer of *Jagdgeschwader* 51 (Pz.Jag./JG 51) was organized in Russia.

In November, 4/Sch.G.2 was posted to North Africa and here, on the hot windblown surface of the desert, the Gnome-Rhone engines proved more vulnerable to the sand than they had to the dust of the Russian Steppes. After only a few sorties, the remaining aircraft were withdrawn from combat to Tripoli where an effective sand filter was quickly designed. However, before any appreciable work could be completed the unit was evacuated to Italy in the face of the Allied offensive in North Africa, and in so doing, destroyed their Hs 129s rather than let them fall into Allied hands.

Anti-Tank Duty

Even with all the 129's shortcomings under combat conditions in both Russia and North Africa, the Luftwaffe pressed ahead with its operational plans (influenced to a great extent by the time period required for a completely new deisgn) equipping further units with the Hs 129 close support aircraft. In December 1942, the 8th *Staffel* of Sch.G.2 based at Tunis-Aounnia received the new plane and in July 1943 was transferred to Russia to join 4/Sch.G.1, 4/Sch.G.2, 8/Sch.G.1 and Pz. Jäg./JG 51. Equipped with the improved Hs 129B-2/R2, which carried a center mounted 30 mm cannon in a ventral pack under the forward fuselage, (scaled up version of a Solothurn 20 mm anti-tank rifle) the *staffels* were assigned specialized anti-tank duty, and on July 8th took part in the German offensive (code named Operation Citadel) against the Soviet spearhead at Kursk. Flying in a shuttle type operation (one unit taking off, one unit attacking the target, one unit returning to base, and one unit rearming and refueling) the Hs 129 enjoyed its greatest single day success, almost singlehandedly repulsing a Russian armored counterattack, destroying the bulk of a Soviet tank brigade (200 vehicles).

In late 1943, the ground attack and close support units of the Luftwaffe were reorganized under General Ernest Kupfer and the five Hs 129 *staffels* were formed into the IV *(Panzer) Gruppe* of *Schlachtgeschwader* 9. This was the only *Gruppe* to include five *Staffels* in the Luftwaffe. In their new organization, the *staffels* were redesignated as shown below:

4 *Staffel*/Sch.G.1	became	10(Pz.) *Staffel*/SG 9
8 *Staffel*/Sch.G.1	became	11(Pz.) *Staffel*/SG 9
4 *Staffel*/Sch.G.2	became	12(Pz.) *Staffel*/SG 9
8 *Staffel*/Sch.G.2	became	13(Pz.) *Staffel*/SG 9
Pz.Jag.*Staffel*/JG 51	became	14(Pz.) *Staffel*/SG 9

The *Gruppe* was then placed under the command of *Hauptmann* (Captain) Bruno Meyer and allowed to freelance over the Eastern Front in search of Soviet armor concentrations and other targets of opportunity, the destruction of which would stall, or slow, the Russian advance. For the next few months the *staffels*, less 11(Pz.)/SG 9 which in October was transferred home to Germany to serve as a test and development unit experimenting with various weapon packages on the Hs 129, served with great success. It was during this time that the Hs 129 finally gained some recognition, admirably performing the assignment it had originally been designed for. Although the radial Gnome-Rhone engines were still sworn at and cursed by the pilots and ground crews, repair procedures had been improved to the point where aircraft downtime was significantly reduced. The Hs 129 continued in action against the Soviet forces through 1944 and into early 1945, when, with the shortage of fuel, the increase in operational losses, and the reduced number of replacement aircraft, it faded from active combat service.

The last Hs 129 variant to see service against the tank forces of the Russian Army was the B3/Wa model which carried a 75 mm BK 7.5 cannon in the ventral pack under the fuselage, replacing the

30 mm cannon usually carried on the B-2 models. The 75 mm gun was the regulation army anti-tank gun stripped of its ground carriage and fitted with a new muzzle brake. Even so, it weighed nearly a ton and fired 12 twenty six pound shells which could penetrate up to four inches of armor plate at 1,000 yards. This particular armament package had been developed and tested by *Erprobungskommando* 26 (Experimental Test unit), formerly 11(Pz.)/SG 9, and proved to be extremely effective against the best armor the Soviet Army had, however, it also proved extremely unwieldy, its rate of fire was slow and with every shot, the recoil caused the aircraft to stagger through the air. In addition the very size of the 75 mm weapon slowed the airspeed of the Hs 129 to a level where it was highly susceptible to both air and ground fire, leading to still greater operational losses.

Near the end of 1944 and into early 1945, the true problems of the Hs 129 were finally given some real attention when experimental installations of new, more powerful engines were made. Unfortunately, the new modifications came about at a time when Allied bombing was halting most of Germany's critical war production machinery, and the change over to a production version of the more powerful Hs 129 never occurred. If it had, especially at an earlier date, the Hs 129 may well have become one of the finest close support aircraft of the war instead of the paradox it turned out to be. With its excellent structural airframe and weapons delivery systems, the Hs 129 was destined, through no fault of its own, for an inglorious and, almost anonymous, place in history by a pair of overrated-underpowered engines. Nevertheless, it was the only successful Axis-built, ground attack aircraft of the entire war.

—Robert Grinsell

Chapter 3
The Do 335 Black Arrow

It was enormous. It sat on the runway like some great prehistoric bird with metal beaks. Ten tons of aluminum, steel, rubber and glass, exuding a biting mixture of oil and gasoline. The time was October, 1943 and the new Dornier Do 335 fighter-bomber had just completed its first flight test successfully.

Considering its speed, dependability and the relative ease with which the prototype transitioned from the experimental to the production stage, the Luftwaffe's decision not to build the brutish Do 335 one year earlier was to cost it dearly.

In 1940 Dr. Claude Dornier had given a practical demonstration of a push-pull design he had patented in 1937. Although tandem fore-and-aft engine arrangements on a center-line thrust axis had been known and used since WW I, it was Dornier who envisioned the push-pull concept in a high speed fighter, with the rear propeller *aft of the tail surfaces*. To prove the practicability of his theory, he and Ulrich Hutter built a small, 22 ft. long flying prototype, equipped with a rear mounted propeller only. Known as the Goppingen Go 9, this lightweight experimental monoplane was powered by an 80 hp. air cooled engine, positioned far forward beneath the shoulder-mounted wing, driving a four-bladed propeller by means of a long extension shaft. Flight tests soon proved the efficiency of the cruciform tail with its additional rudder and fin, which gave the aircraft exemplary stability and handling. The small Hirth engine drove the Go 9 to a remarkable top speed of 137 mph. and the long extension shaft proved not only workable, but sturdy and reliable.

With an additional engine mounted forward, both of which would be at least 20 times more powerful, Dornier began design work on a full size fighter capable of speeds over 450 mph. Unfortunately for him, but fortunately for the Western Allies, the Luftwaffe was not interested. France had just been blitzed in a six week walkover, England would soon follow suit. The warplanes the Reich already had on inventory and in the jigs, were considered sufficient to make Germany master of Europe. Thus, the summer of 1940 came and went. Dornier shuffled paper and made a few additional proposals the following year, but although several department heads in the Bureau of Technical Procurement seemed interested, Dornier was firmly informed that Dornier A.G. was to stick to bombers and flying boats.

The year 1941 did not bring victory to Germany and early in 1942, almost two years after Dornier's program could have been put into effect, the Luftwaffe finally decided to look into the possible benefits of acquiring a single-seat, unarmed, high-speed intruder capable of carrying a half ton of bombs at 495 mph.

Delays

Junkers and Arado also submitted deisgns, but Dornier's push-pull fighter, with its cruciform tail, was clearly superior and was awarded the contract. Once given the green light, Dornier's engineers delivered a prototype ready for testing, nine months after the first metal was cut. During the interim, however, several factors combined to further delay and hamper the program. The Luftwaffe had gone over to the defensive during 1942. Instead of bombers, it now needed tactical aircraft, high speed fighter-bombers, reconnaissance aircraft, heavy fighters or destroyers, and all weather interceptors. Dornier's new aircraft could be any or all of these, given time for reconfiguring, but there was no time, and after the Dornier design team has finished the original unarmed intruder blueprints, the thrust of the project was abruptly changed because of the new, defensively oriented requirements. Dornier made the required adjustments, but more lead time had slipped away, precious months that could never be recouped. Thus, instead of the Do 335 prototype flying in October, 1942, it flew for the first time exactly one year later (Fig. 3-1).

Had Lufwaffe procurement been more alert to their changing needs, and given Dornier a contract in the fall of 1940 on the basis of the Go 9, the Do 335 *Pfeil* (Arrow) could have flown in the summer of 1941, and been in production, in great numbers, by the fall of the following year (Fig. 3-2). The summer of 1943, which marked the beginning of heavy Allied Bombing raids over the Reich, would have seen it stocking almost all interceptor *ges-*

Fig. 3-1. Like a tamed predator, the second of ten Do 335A pre-production fighter-bombers is seen on the hardstand at Pautuxent Naval Air Station where it was evaluated after the war.

chwaders in the Reich, in both its day and night fighter versions, and the battle for air superiority over Europe may have gone very differently.

What Might Have Been

This analysis of what might have been is not limited to the Dornier 335, of course. The first jet interceptor, the Messerschmitt 262, ran a similar course of misplaced emphasis, production delays and chronic vacillation. And while it is true that Junkers did not perfect the turbojet which powered it until the fall of 1944, thus denying large scale production, it is equally true that had the Do 335 program been brought to fruition when it was ready, the appearance of German jet aircraft in early 1945 would have been on terms far more favorable than those encountered by the few pilots who manned them during the Luftwaffe's last death throes.

With the Dornier Do 335 in squadron service by the summer of 1943, with a still largely untouched war machine functioning solidly behind it, the Germans would have possessed the fastest, most powerfully armed fighters and fighter-bombers of the war. Big, strong and reliable, the Do 335 proved itself a versatile design. It had the load-carrying and range of a fighter-bomber, the speed and altitude of a pure interceptor and the size and firepower necessary for specialized night-fighting. It was extremely maneuverable and its very configuration allowed it to carry all types of specialized gear, from sophisticated radar antenna arrays to special bombs. A

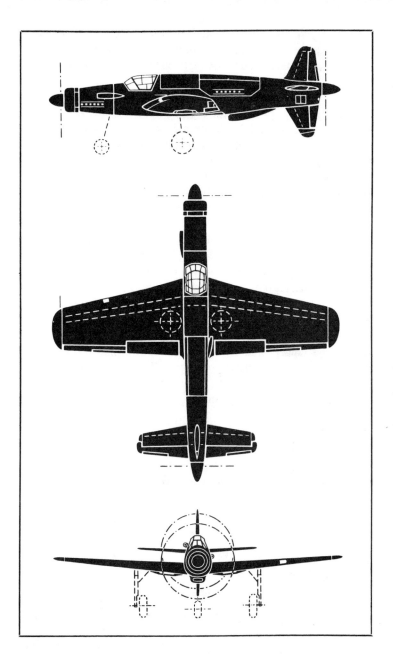

Fig. 3-2. Three view of the single-seat version of the Do 335 Pfeil (Arrow). Twin push-pull engines produced a maximum of 3,600 horsepower to give this exciting interceptor a maximum speed above 470 mph.

particularly stable gun platform, it would have been a natural as a rocket launcher, and its rugged durability was proven when test models flew at pseeds up to 350 mph. on the rear engine alone (Fig. 3-3).

All of the foregoing, however, is pure conjecture. Never given a particularly high priority, the Arrow lauguished. The only combat it was destined to see was with a special *kommando* formed in September, 1944, which used ten pre-production A-O models to develop tactics for the new fighter. Results of encounters with Allied aircraft are sketchy, but French ace, Pierre Clostermann, reports sighting what could only have been a Do 335 in the late fall of 1944.

Viewed from a perspective of 30 years hindsight, the Do 335 had everything going for it. Its engine was the reliable Daimler Benz 603E-1 (Fig. 3-4), a variation of the standard classic that had propelled the Luftwaffe to preeminence during the first two years of the war. In fact, the engine's reliability may have hurt the Arrow program, since so many other German aircraft builders were struggling to obtain it for their own planes. Ironically enough, the only fatality which occurred during the Do 335 test program, was due to the failure of the rear DB 603 powerplant. The second prototype crashed and was a total writeoff, when it suddenly burst into flame. This was the one accident in the entire program, a record that few aircraft can match.

Pilots Praise

Luftwaffe test pilots who flew the Arrow were full of praise for its handling characteristics. Its turning circle was very small and the few night-fighter veterans who took it up, were convinced that

Fig. 3-3. Weighing more than nine tons and with provision for an internal bomb bay or extra fuel tankage, the Arrow should have excelled in almost any tactical role.

28

Fig. 3-4. The Arrow's engines were the reliable Daimler Benz 603 of 1,800 hp. inverted V-12s.

they would now be able to counteract the nocturnal raids by the British Mosquito (Fig. 3-5). The Do 335 was roomy enough to carry all the latest radar and night-fighting equipment. With its bombbay removed, it could carry an additional 200 gallons of fuel. Its sturdy overall structure easily allowed the installation of 30mm Mk 103 cannon in the wings, firing 70 rounds each at a rate of better than ten shots per second Fig. 3-6). With an exceptional cruise of 281 mph. the Do 335 had an excellent loiter time factor, giving it a range of 1,305 miles. Its stability would have made it an excellent close support aircraft and its ability to top 350 mph. on one engine gave it an edge in durability over more vulnerable Luftwaffe tactical types.

In addition to performance and pusher configuration, the Do 335 was an innovative machine in many other respects. The crew was provided with ejection seats, the first introduced. The upper tail surfaces and propeller could be jettisoned by means of explosive bolts, allowing the pilot to clear the empennage and blades behind him. And the Do 335 was the first German figher to incorporate a tricycle landing gear. Despite this configuration, pilots were instructed to land tail down, taking the initial shock on the main gear, before allowing the nose to droop. In a wheels up landing, the lower fin and rudder could also be jettisoned (Fig. 3-7).

About the only fault pilots found with the Arrow or Anteater, as they preferred to call it, was its poor rearward vision. But this deficiency was somewhat overcome by molding bulges into the side of the canopy and equipping them with rear view mirrors.

Faster Than Black Widow

It is one of the constant ironies of war that the best weaponry is not always that requested by the decision-makers in charge of procurement. This myopic outlook is largely due to misinformation, lack of funds, incorrect prognosis and inability to produce and deliver. In the case of the Do 335 it was due mainly to sloth. The

Fig. 3-5. The Arrow was a big airplane and carefully planned. Pilots liked its maneuverability and ease of handling. Fortunately for the Allies, the German Air Ministry, for whatever reasons, did not expedite its production.

Fig. 3-6. Do 335 interceptor carried a pair of 30-mm Mk 103 cannons in its wings, each firing 70 rounds per minute. Pilot was provided with an ejection seat.

Fig. 3-7. Nose wheel and strut detail.

Dornier Do 335 A-6 „Pfeil" Nachtjäger

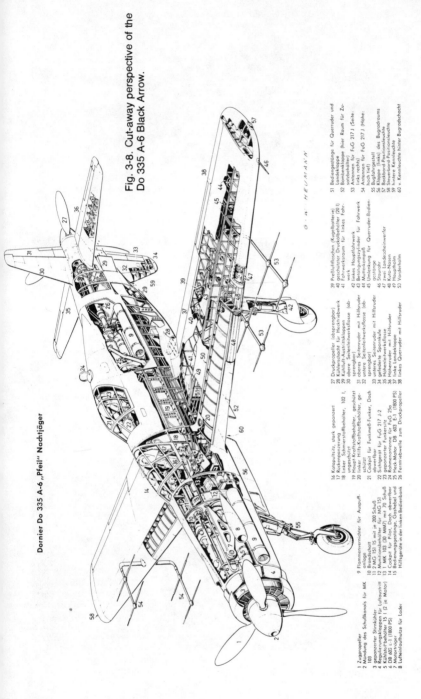

Fig. 3-8. Cut-away perspective of the Do 335 A-6 Black Arrow.

G. R. HEUMANN

1 Zugpropeller
2 Mündung des Schußkanals für MK
3 gepanzerter Stirnkühler
4 Regulierungsklappen für Luftaustritt
5 Kühlstoffkühler I (2 je Motor)
6 DB 603 i.-1 (1800 PS)
7 Motorträger
8 Lufteinlaufschütze für Lader
9 Flammenvernichter für Auspuff-
   anlage
10 Brandschott
11 2 MG 151 15 mit je 200 Schuß
12 Munitionsbehälter für MG 151
13 1 MK 103 (MK?) mit 70 Schuß
14 Cockpit für Pilot, Dach abwerfbar
15 Bedienungsgestänge, Gashebel und
   Hilfsgeräte in der linken Bedienbank

16 Katapultsitz, stark gepanzert
17 Rückenpanzerung
18 linker Schmierstoffbehälter, 102 l,
   ungeschützt
19 Haupt-Kraftstoffbehälter, geschützt
20 linker Hilfs-Kraftstoffbehälter, geschützt
21 Cockpit für Funkmeß-Funker, Dach
   abwerfbar
22 Sichtgerät für FuG 217 J-2
23 gepanzerter Funkersitz
24 Rahmenantenne für FuG 25a
25 Heck-Motor DB 603 E-1 (1800 PS)
26 Fernantriebswelle zum Druckpropeller

27 Druckpropeller (absprengbar)
28 Kühlerschacht für Hecktriebwerk
29 Kühlluft-Austrittsklappen
30 obere Seitenschwerksflosse (absprengbar)
31 oberes Seitenruder mit Hilfsruder
32 untere Seitenschwerksflosse (absprengbar)
33 unteres Seitenruder mit Hilfsruder
34 gefederte Spornkufe
35 Höhenleitwerksflosse
36 Höhenruder mit Hilfsruder
37 linke Landeklappe
38 linkes Querruder mit Hilfsruder

39 Preßluftflaschen (Kugelbatterie)
40 geschützter Druckölbehälter (20 l)
41 Fahrwerkraum für linkes Fahrwerk
42 linkes Hauptfahrwerk
43 Betätigungszylinder für Fahrwerk
44 Anlenkung für Fahrwerk
45 Umlenkung für Querruder-Bedien-
   gestänge
46 Staurohr
47 zwei Landescheinwerfer
48 Koto-Nasen
49 Hauptholm
50 Vorderholm

51 Bediengestänge für Querruder und
   Landeklappe
52 Bombenklappe (hier Raum für Zu-
   satzbehälter)
53 Antennen für FuG 217 J (Seite:
   links rechts)
54 Antennen für FuG 217 J (Höhe:
   hoch tief)
55 Bugfahrgestell
56 Klappe (links) des Bugradraums
57 Backbord Positionsleuchte
58 Steuerbord Positionsleuchte
59 hintere Kennleuchte
60 v. Kennleuchte hinter Bugradschacht

32

plane was available, its design was proven, and it could have easily been built in quantity had the powers-that-be understood what it was . . . potentially the finest piston-engined fighter of WW II. It certainly would have ranked with the Mosquito and the Mustang. If one needs an Allied fighter to compare it with for speed, size, firepower and performance, it could be said that it was similar to the Northrop P-61 Black Widow, except for the fact that it was 100 mph. faster and had far greater range.

In the east, it was a natural for the low-level destroyer role the Wehrmacht needed to blunt Russian tank thrusts. Its speed and performance, even with one engine out, was tailor-made for ground support, where attacking aircraft are forced to brave intense anti-aircraft fire. Since its landing speed was no higher than that of the light Fw 190 (110 mph.) it could have operated from even the most makeshift Russian fighter bases. Yet it would have been far more versatile. With three times the range and four times the ammunition capacity, the Do 335 B single-seat model could have literally ruled the air over the front and even struck deeply behind the Russian lines, something the Fw 190 could not do.

As an all weather fighter and night interceptor, the Do 335 A two-seater, possessed all the requirements for carrying advanced weapons systems and search radar, at both high speeds (428 mph.) and high altitude (34,000 ft.) (Fig. 3-8). As a day interceptor, the faster (475 mph.) single seat B model would have held the great Allied bomber streams in check with its pair of 30mm wing cannon, which could have been augmented with an additional 30mm nose cannon, as well as rockets. As a fast attack bomber, the Do 335 A-1, could carry a ton of bombs, half internally, half externally, and fly a 500 mile combat radius.

To be sure, the Dornier Do 335 did not represent a panacea for the problems which beset the Luftwaffe in the summer of 1943. At war's end, little of the performance enumerated above was realized beyond the boundaries of the testing grounds. With the Reich crumbling under air attack, production dried up in a shortage of parts, trained labor and fuel. The time, manpower and facilities wasted in producing Junkers Ju 87 Stukas and Messerschmitt 110, 210 and 410s long beyond their usefulness, could not be transferred to the Dornier program. The fighter that might have won the air war for Germany could not be resurrected.

−Karl Toll

Chapter 4
Defending the Reich
Against the Americans

Note: Except for the Battle of Britain, no Allied fighter pilots had to undergo the strain of protecting a modern industrial state against determined air attack. Only the Luftwaffe's fighter command was faced with that ordeal and, unlike the relatively short summer challenge faced by the RAF, their unenviable task lasted more than two full years of near round the clock bombing. Survivors of that monumental assignment are rare. Rarer still are the few willing to talk about it. Lt. Franz Stigler is one of them, a 28 victory ace with JG 27, he was already an experienced pilot when he started flying combat, with the benefit of three years flights instruction behind him. His observations on the air war in the skies over Western and Southern Europe are both compelling and informative, the product of having experienced, firsthand, the greatest air battles ever fought.□

The Luftwaffe's fighter arm began life under a clandestine cloud of secrecy. Forbidden by the Treaty of Versailles to possess an air force, it sent its pilots to Russia for training during the late twenties and early thirties, until the strained relations between Germany and the Soviets forced the program to be discontinued. Between 1933 and 1935, aspiring pilots received their training at "commercial flying schools" in Germany, under the tutelage of veteran First World War pilots. Most of them had been flying gliders since their teens, and by the time they reached these thinly disguised flying schools, were well grounded in the rudiments of flight.

In the mid-thirties, Germany's new ally, Mussolini's Italy, opened its facilities to groups of selected German pilots, and by 1935 there was no need to continue the charade. Germany was rearming. Her factories were turning out new warplanes and she openly conducted flying training at her own combat fighter schools. Adolph Hitler may have been defying the Treaty of Versailles, but the Western Allies were doing very little about it.

With the outbreak of the Spanish Civil War in the summer of 1936, Germany was ready to test some of her new equipment, along with several theories her military staff had developed. Foremost among these was that of aerial bombardment, particularly close support tactics. During the Spanish Civil War, the Germans were guilty of many blunders, one of them being the indiscriminate bombing of non military targets. Much of this unwanted reputation was due to the policies of Herman Goering who envisioned the bomber as a terror weapon by which whole populations could be bludgeoned into capitulation. His leader, Hitler, was also convinced that this was the correct approach. Both were proven wrong.

In Spain, indiscriminate bombing of civilian targets by German and Nationalist forces only resulted in bad publicity. During the Battle of Britain, three years later, it stiffened the will of the British people to resist, and when the Allies utilized it later on in the war in colossal raids that wiped out entire cities, German morale did not break. Instead of crushing the home front, such raids only fueled the enemy's spirit to fight back, and the atomic bomb excepted, World War II proved that the civilian population only collapsed when their field armies were already beaten.

However, the Luftwaffe learned one important tactical lesson during its interlude with Spain. Close air support not only insured the success of an attack, but could also be used in repelling an enemy thrust. Assigned as the commander of Number 3 Staffel of the Luftwaffe's Condor Legion Wing 88, Adolf Galland learned to use the obsolete Heinkel He 51 biplane fighter as a fighter/bomber on the northern front with good results.

Inferior to the Russian-built Republican fighters it was forced to face, Galland employed his aircraft in the close support role, attacking enemy infantry in low-flying sorties. The light bombs they carried (110 lb.) were small by later standards, but they were pwoerful enough to break up troop concentrations, soft-skinned vehicles and the lightly armored tanks and scout cars of the period. The Heinkel He 51 made its operational debut in Spain in the fall of 1936, when three dozen were despatched with the first Condor Legion volunteers. Disguised as tourists, visiting professors, athletes and the like, a ploy which was used by both sides, volunteer German, Italian, American, French and Russian pilots

Fig. 4-1. Messerschmitt 109E-3 in factory markings. Camouflage scheme is typical of summer 1940, with light blue undersurfaces carried two-thirds of the way up the fuselage. Top is two-tone dark green and black-green splinter pattern.

swarmed into the country to flesh out the air arms of the belligerents.

By the end of 1937, however, it was clear that the Nationalists had the upper hand. The flow of Russian equipment to the Republican forces had been greatly diminished and the Nationalists now had control of the air. With the introduction into combat that summer of the Messerschmitt 109B, it was only a matter of time before the combined air forces of Germany, Italy and the Nationalists achieved complete air superiority (Fig. 4-1). Where Adolf Galland and his He 51 biplane had to rely on maximum use of the Heinkel's best features to provide an effective air weapon, the Condor Legion-bolstered Nationalists now had the finest fighter in the air. They also were using their new Messerschmitt fighter in a completely new and innovative way.

Same Tactics

The Civil War in Spain picked up where combat had left off twenty years before. The weapons were more modern, particularly the aircraft involved, but the tactics were the same on both sides, based on the other static lessons learned above the trenches of WWI. Where Galland used his obsolescent Heinkels as flying artillery, concentrating them at key points, Werner Moelders, his successor as the commander of Squadron 3, rewrote the book of fighter tactics.

He was aided immeasurably by the introduction of the superior 109C which began replacing the older Heinkel 51, two months after Moelders took command of the squadron. The debut of this fleet, low-wing, modern monoplane, which was approximately 100 mph. faster than the Heinkel and equipped with radio and oxygen, opened up a host of new potentialities which could be achieved in the air. With a fast, heavily armed fighter, armed with four 7.9 machine guns, the Condor Legion now had a weapon which the Republicans did not possess. The fabric covered Polikarpov I-15 biplane wilted under its guns, and as long as the 109 did not engage in the old fashioned dogfight, its more nimble opponent had little or no chance against it. Even the faster I-16 *Mosca* monoplane

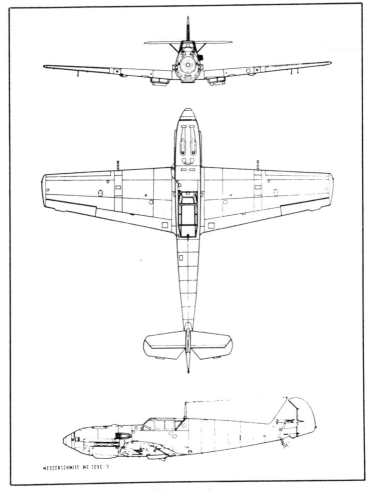

MESSERSCHMITT ME 109E-3

Fig. 4-2. Messerschmitt Me 109E-3 three-view.

fighter, although more maneuverable, did not have the equipment possessed by the new 109 and Moelders was not slow in developing tailor made techniques to take better advantage of his superior fighter (Fig. 4-2).

It may be fairly said that the aerial tactics developed by Moelders in Spain were to form the basic principles for Luftwaffe fighter pilots throughout the war.

Because the 109 was well armed, fast and could dive quickly and climb well, Moelders developed the slash and recover method of attack. In it, German pilots would pick out their target, dive, fire and recover, climbing back up again for another attack. They were not to involve themselves in a close aerial melee of constantly turning aircraft. The idea was to hit hard and hit first from an advantageous position. Aerobatic exhibitions of fancy flying were discouraged. These could be engaged in when the pilot had no other choice. But if Moelders' rules were followed his pilots would have that choice. He would initiate the attack. He would break it off. The fighting would be over ground of his choosing. To be able to do this, one needed a superior aircraft and in the 109, the Germans had it. When, in 1943, they lost this superiority, they were forced to rely on experience to make up for what they lacked in equipment and numbers, and this latter necessity became the story of the Luftwaffe through the end of the war. In Spain, however, German pilots had the planes, the numbers and, most important, the leaders and the correct strategy.

New Formation

Provided with the best weaponry, Moelders quickly evolved a new tactical formation, known to the Germans as the *rotte*. Simply stated this was the beginning of the two-ship element of leader and wing man which forms the basis for all fighter pilot techniques. Usually paired up in a grouping of two *rottes* forming a *schwarm*, this formation is similar to the four fingers of the extended hand. It is versatile, inherently strong and, more important, natural. In it, the leader of each *rotte* initiates the attack, while his wing man covers his rear and protects him, allowing him to concentrate on the enemy. Meanwhile, one *rotte* covers the other, flying in a staggered position, one above and one below.

Simplicity is the prime asset of this formation of four. It is self protecting and even when broken down to its smallest element, the *rotte*, still contains the basics of attack and defense. When used on a larger scale, one squadron will fly cover for another, but within each squadron of 12 aircraft, the six two-ship elements within will still be self supporting and self sustaining, even as they afford mutual support to each other.

The introduction of the *rotte* and the *schwarm* were the direct antithesis of what had been learned and practiced during the First World War. Then aerial combat had begun with the lone wolf sortie, gradually increasing to gaggles of aircraft, all flying in a huge buzzing mass, much like a swarm of stinging insects. From these had developed the aerial circuses, named as much for their spectacular dogfighting free-for-alls, as their gaudily painted aircraft. Despite the great number of aces and their incredible victory strings, little scientific planning had been injected into aerial combat, and even as WW I drew to a close, the lone wolf was still the pivotal fighter around whom combat revolved.

Moelders changed all this and in the change he established a number of new realities. The modern fighter was fast enough and flew high enough to cover a great deal more area, particularly with the advent of radio. Packing aircraft in tightly, in clumsy formations, not only made for a vulnerable target, by reducing maneuvering room, but sharply restricted the area a fighter squadron could sweep. By limiting a unit's range of action, its effectiveness was curtailed, merely by halving the opportunities it would have to meet the enemy. Pilots which did not see combat because they were unable to extend their aircraft over the fullest range, were wasted, as was their gunpower. However, the Moelders' new tactical formation, the Luftwaffe received the maximum from its men and machines.

British and French Slow To Change

While Moelders was drilling his new tactics into the men who would become the squadron, group and wing leaders of WW II, the British and the French were still clinging to the old concepts of WW I. The British, especially, were slow to jettison their time-honored tactics, time-honored because they had proven successful in another war. They still flew in old line abreast and line astern formations, much of the time in squadron size. This meant at least twelve aircraft following their leader in a single line, with the leader either high or low, and leading a group which was echeloned either to the left or right. This put all of a squadron's aircraft together and when it broke to join combat, all followed the leader in line, hampering maneuverability. Only on patrol sweeps of two aircraft did the British follow the German *rotte* principle, and this

Fig. 4-3. A German fighter pilot of JG 26 scans the sky across the English Channel for Allied aircraft. The Messerschmitt 109E had performance very close to the Spitfire during the Battle of Britain, but its pair of wing-mounted 20-mm cannon were effective at greater ranges than the Spit's rifle-caliber guns. The F model, which followed in 1941, was probably the best of the series, the G model being so over-gunned that performance suffered.

was only due to the fact that there was no other choice. Unfortunately, the British did not realize the fundamental benefits of the *rotte* until the end of 1940, when R.A.F. pilots who practiced it by necessity during the Battle of Britain informed their superiors of its inherent superiority (Fig. 4-3).

France's Army of the Air began experimenting with the two-ship element in 1939, learning from the lessons of the Spanish war, and on the days when the French Air Force could field enough fighters during the Battle of France, managed to punish the Luftwaffe in fighter to fighter combat. Although the Army of the Air was caught in the middle of a conversion program when the Luftwaffe struck in May, 1940, its pilots were of extremely high quality, and its slower Morane 406 fighters were very maneuverable. A great many Luftwaffe pilots, Moelders among them, temporarily forgot the lessons taught in Spain (Fig. 4-4) Amid the heady wine of smashing victory, they were shot down by French pilots who lured them into one-on-one turning dogfights. Trained in the old school of dogfighting, as were the Italians and the Japanese, and flying aircraft which excelled in such maneuvers, the French claimed Moelders himself, as well as Egon Mayer, who went on to down 102 Allied aircraft, including 25 four engined

B-24s and B-17s. However, once France surrendered, the captured Luftwaffe aces their pilots had shot down were released to fight again .

Meanwhile in America, a fighter formation similar to the German *rotte* had been developed simultaneously. Known in the U.S. Air Corps as the "tactical two," consisting of a leader and his wing man, it was being practiced as early as 1938. However, the Air Corps was so short of modern pursuit planes, that its fighter pilots were flying three and four different types of aircraft, including bombers, to get their full allotment of flying time. Furthermore, American pilots were still dogfighting once they engaged, and this tactic was to produce terrible consequences once U.S. pilots met the Japanese Zero.

New Phase

The year 1941 saw the air war in Europe enter a new phase. Gone were the big bomber raids by the Luftwaffe against England. Fighter combat was marked primarily by the clash of patrols on sweeps over the Channel Coast and became a deadly game of experts who knew their machines extremely well. Thus the war in the skies marked time until 1943 and the advent of the big bomber raids. Then an altogether different type of warfare began, one which pitted masses of interceptors against armadas of heavy bombers and their escorts. In the skies over Europe during the years 1944-1945, the dogfight was eclipsed by the need to stop the bombers at all costs.

Fig. 4-4. Damaged in combat, this Me 109 crash landed in Southern France, 1944, and was stripped of its wheels and guns. Many writers today refer to these aircraft as "Bf 109s," because the design originated with Bayerisch-fleugzuegwerke, the Bavarian Aircraft Works, in 1935. At that time, Willy Messerschmitt was chief of design for that company—which became a subsidiary of Messerschmitt A.G. in 1938. Most American pilots who met them in combat, referred to them as "Me 109s."

The Luftwaffe came to know the Boeing B-17 intimately. In the air they credited it with speed, load carrying, ruggedness and bristling defensive firepower. They shot down over 4,000 of them in combat and several of these landed virtually intact. Carefully refurbished, they were placed at the disposal fo ZS-1 or Destroyer School I, operated by German air intelligence, and used by them to instruct German fighter pilots on the best method of attacking the Fortress.

As has already been noted, the B-17's most vulnerable quarter of attack was from headon, until the advent of the G model with its twin-gunned chin turret. The next best option was straight down from directly above and a bit behind, but such technique called for precision flying, and in 1944-45, Luftwaffe fighter pilot ranks were filled mostly by inexperienced cadets fresh out of flying school. Because they lacked experience, this left only the mass headon attacks, as practiced by the *Rammkommando* units or the beam attack, launched at a 45 degree angle from above.

The latter had the advantage of placing the vulnerable oil tanks, inside of the inboard nacelles, and the wing fuel tanks, inside of the outboard nacelles, directly in the attackers' path, for the B-17 had little protective armor itself. In addition to armored seat backs, only the metal surrounding the waist gun cut-outs was reinforced with steel plate, as was the bulkhead separating the top turret gunner's compartment from the bomb bay. The firewall dividing the pilots from the navigator's station was also armored to a lesser extent. The nose section of the B-17 didn't even have a steel deck for the bombardier and the navigator and, frequently, the entire compartment could be blown off, with the bomber continuing to fly. To kill the B-17 in its body, one had to break the integrity of the flight deck, or explode its bombs in the bay. Anything less only damaged the bomber. B-17s came back from missions nearly torn in two at the waist, but still flyable. If hit in any number of non vital parts, including the rudder, the big Fortress might lose airspeed, struggle and trail smoke, but it would continue on course. Consolidated B-24 Liberators frequently blew up when hit. The B-17 rarely did. Therefore, in order to destroy it, German pilots were trained to attack the B-17's cabin and its wing and oil tanks.

Attacking a formation from the rear was foolhardy, due to the converging fire from the bomber's tail and ball turret batteries. Tail attacks provided the oncoming fighters a longer closure time in which to line up on target, but even as they did so, they were peppered by a veritable barrage of twin .50 caliber machine gun fire.

Lt. Franz Stigler of JG 27, who was to be shot down an incredible 17 times, during the course of some 500 missions, describes what it was like attacking B-17s during the Defense of the Reich in 1944-45.

"At first, the unescorted bombers were relatively easy to destroy and suffered prohibitive losses. When the P-47s and P-38s began escorting them part way, early in 1944, we had to alter our method of attack, but as soon as they left, due to lack of fuel, we pounded the bombers unmercifully. Our interception time was more limited than it had been in late 1943, but our technique had improved so that we were able to accomplish more in less time. Our ground control methods were also better and we could now call in interceptors from a far larger area."

A Memorable Attack

"The intervening years have tended to blur my combat missions together, but one attack against the bombers stands out in my memory. It was early 1944 and an unescorted formation of B-17s came up from the Mediterranean to bomb Germany. Our group (36 aircraft) was ordered off to intercept, with my squadron flying high cover to ward off any escorting fighters, while the other two went after the bombers. We made contact just north of the Alps, a few miles from Munich. No escorting fighters were around and I radioed the group commander, informing him that he could attack at will."

"For some reason, unknown to me, the group commander ignored my information. The other two squadrons continued to fly around the bomber formation of approximately 100 planes, just out of range. Finally, after repeated calls to my commander, and furious because we were allowing a prize opportunity to slip through our fingers, I initiated the attack."

"To this day, I do not know why the group commander refused to attack. Several combat leaders, after they had won the Swords or Diamonds to their Knight's Cross, stopped flying combat, perhaps believing that they could do no more, particularly after they had been awarded the Diamonds, but this was not the case in this instance. At any rate, we had a good chance to inflict maximum damage to the Fortresses below us and I led my twelve plane squadron down in a screaming dive."

"We flashed past the high combat box in an overhead pass,

continuning on through in a breakaway, before climbing back up for another attack."

"With no escort fighters to challenge us, we swept through the B-17 formation five times. Twenty-four of them sagged from their boxes and although we suffered hits, not one fighter was lost and no pilots were even scratched. Three of our pilots were on their first combat mission and this attack was a remarkable boost to their morale, providing them with a type of indoctrination not many new pilots would ever live to see."

"In addition to our success, the attack impressed upon me the absolutely critical need for fighter escort which even heavily armed bombers like the B-17 required. In the ensuing months I learned the hard way never to attack a heavy bomber from the rear, even though the Luftwaffe high command gave out orders stating this was the best way to do the job . . . that is at first. Experience soon proved that the concentrated fire from the tail cone .50 caliber weapons was brought to bear best when fighters came in from this angle. After following orders and being shot down several times, I decided to go in from above whenever possible. With high speed built up in a dive, my aircraft made a very fleeting target and the more vertical my descent, the more difficult it was for the top turret gunner to get an angle on me. Most of the time I was through the formation before he even saw me and would be climbing back up for another pass."

"On this type of approach, the firing time allotted to me was extremely limited. I could get in only one short burst. But I was going so fast that I was also harder to hit, and the real danger in this type of pass was that I might collide with my quarry. Nevertheless, I would rather make several high speed vertical passes, getting in only a short burst each time, than come in from the rear with all the tail gunners of one box shooting at me during a prolonged approach."

"When diving down from above, a few hits from your 20mm cannon was all that was necessary. Your target was usually made up of the pilots' cabin, the engines and the wing's oil and fuel tanks. When you came in from the rear, you saw mostly rudder; the B-17's wings were presented to you in their narrowest aspect. If you came in a trifle low, you received ball turret fire. If too high, the top turret gunner could track you very well and you also received fire from the radio hatch gun. On the breakaway, the waist gunners could also get in a few parting shots. Diving from above really eliminated a great deal of the enemy's potential for defense. In many instances you were going so fast, his top gunner never saw you, and if he did, it was difficult for him to fire straight up. The target the B-17 or B-24 presented in this attitude was the widest possible and after making your pass, you could usually break past without any other guns, from the ship being attacked, shooting at you. Guns from bombers on either side, however, could reach you quite well, but here again your speed aided you, and as you approached their sistership, fire would have to be withheld for fear of hitting their own bomber. However, as I have said before, in this type of attack the closure rate was frightening. The target appeared almost stationary and loomed up at you like a concrete runway. Your firing time was perhaps 1/5 that of the tail approach and you really had to break off quickly. Nevertheless, it had one great compensation, when you were firing at your bomber he, more often than not, wasn't firing back at you. Before the coming of the chin-turreted bombers, a headon pass was a good choice, if you broke down low, but they could see you coming from a long way out, and you could be hit by other ships in the formation."

"By the spring of 1944 all our 109s and 190s were heavily armored. With the introduction of wing cannon in the 109, our old fighter became a truck. I refused to fly it with the additional 20mm cannon slung in pods under the wing. The extra guns were good against bombers, but greatly hampered lateral control, cut speed significantly and because of the high loads encountered, often jammed. Worst of all, when we met escorting fighters of any kind, and P-51 Mustangs in particular, we were at a mortal disadvantage. It was worth your life to be caught flying a 109 with wing cannon against a Mustang and most of the pilots in my squadron elected to stick with the 109G-6 with its two 13mm cowl guns and a single G 151 20mm cannon firing through the propeller hub."

"In mid 1944, we were offered the Fw 190. It was a good aircraft and they had beefed it up with a great deal of armor plate. Some carried their 20mm cannon (four of them) in underwing trays, while others were fitted with larger 30mm types in big gondolas, outboard of their 20mm weapons. Because of their armament, these aircraft were to be used to attack the bombers while we took on the escorts."

"Personally, I preferred the older 109. The Fw 190 was easy to fly. Visibility was good and the wide gear made taking off and landing far more pleasant than in the 109. The cockpit was roomy and comfortable. Control layout was better than in the 109 and the whole aircraft was less cramped. The 190 also had little sophisticated touches, such as electric trim tabs. It was light on the controls, and it could really turn, much better than the 109. This was one quality which the 190 was not given proper credit for. It could also flip over very quickly and dive, and its top speed was faster than that of the 109. Although later variants were much improved, at altitudes, above 25,000 ft. the 190's performance fell off sharply and the 109 was the superior fighter."

Living conditions for pilots remained good throughout the war, for those stationed in Germany, but Franz recalls that this had not always been the case elsewhere.

"I was never in Russia, but in the desert we lived like animals. Down there at the end of a long supply line, our food was monotonous at best, usually combat rations and there was no such things as fresh meat or milk. Water was scarce and had to be used for military purposes. We rarely bathed unless we were near the ocean. We lived in holes in the ground, dug-outs, with canvas pulled over them. The sand was everywhere; in our eyes, ears, mouth, food, water, our airplanes. The desert was a sort of forgotten war and like our comarades in the panzer units, we got whatever was left over from other theaters."

"It was the same with the British too. Their equipment was also second class and it wasn't until late 1941 that we began to see Spitfires. In the desert we were always badly outnumbered, at all times. It seems that our high command had the idea that the Italian air force would be able to take up the slack and implement our meager supplies. Such was not the case. Most of their aircraft were usually down for repair due to the fact they were not equipped with sand filters, even though an Italian designed filter equipped our fighters, and a great deal of their first line strength was made up of outmoded biplanes. These were very maneuverable and their pilots were extremely good, but they just didn't have the speed to match the British Hurricanes and American-built P-40s. I remember that some of the Italians used to turn into hurricane attacks, firing their cowl mounted .50 caliber guns in an attempt to hit the enemy at long range, before his less powerful .30 caliber weapons could be brought to bear. This was the only way they could compete. When the cannon armed Hurricane was introduced, they had no chance at all. We saw very little of the more modern Italian fighters such as the Macchi 200 and 202. When we did, they also were usually in the repair sheds. But I will say something for the Italian pilots, they liked to mix it up and excelled at dogfighting."

"When we retreated to Italy, the food and quarters got better and the nearer we got to home, the better living conditions became. In Germany, we had the best of everything. The poor civilians were suffering, of course, and we were eating *ersatz* everything, but we pilots lived well. We had fresh eggs, coffee, milk, cigarettes, even beer and liquor. Fresh beef and pork were scarce, but we easily supplemented this with horsemeat.

"I remember one station near Nuremberg where we were billeted in private homes. Before dawn, we would go out to the airfield in trucks and stop off at a horse butcher who was open and buy sausage and salami made of horsemeat, riding the rest of the way to the field chewing our breakfast."

"Actually the shortage that we could never overcome was that of fuel. About mid 1944, the lack of aviaiton gas and our losses in experienced pilots became very evident in the quality of the replacements we were sent. The shortage of fuel was dictating a drastically reduced flying course. New pilots came to use with but the most rudimentary notion of aerobatics and practically no instrument time. Instead of having 400 or 500 hours, many had only 150. Primary training was 30 or 40 hours, after which the cadet moved up to heavier aircraft for formation flying, but it was the rare replacement who had been given even ten hours in a 109 before being sent into combat."

"I really worried about these kids and along with most responsible squadron commanders tried to bring them along slowly, but the war would not always wait. Giving them a chance to break in gradually was nearly impossible and I can remember that terrible feeling I got when I was forced to have them fly combat before they were anywhere near ready, for I well recall how green I was during my first combat and I had several thousand hours of flying time."

"As time went on the problem grew worse. They came to us with practically nothing. In late 1944, we got some of them into the squadron with less than 150 hours of total flying time and only four or five hours on 109s. What can you do with kids like that?"

"We tried to save them, but we just had to take them along on missions because there just weren't enough pilots to fill out the group. Many of them were lost the first time up. They would simply freeze and just sit there while P-51s and P-47s shot them to pieces. They didn't know what to do."

"Some were lucky and were able to bail out or crash land safely. Usually the experience made them better pilots on their next flights, but because of their basic lack of time and experience, they were quickly shot down again and very few survived. New replacements were usually gone in a few days or a week at most, before we even got to know them and in order to keep my own sanity, I tried not to, even though my instincts told me to protect them as best I could."

"There was really very little I could do. We used to hope for bad weather, so we wouldn't have to fly and could rest. Even in the winter of 1944-1945 when the days were short, we would fly two, three, four missions per day. The pressure was unbearable. We became sick with fatigue and on several occasions I had to be lifted out of my cockpit when returning from the third or fourth mission of the day. Often pilots would fall asleep with their engines ticking over, waiting to go up. We were being beaten both physically and psychologically, literally hammered to destruction."

"During this time, most of the pilots shot down by Allied fighters were inexperienced recruits. Once in a while an old hand's luck would run out, usually when we tried to go to the aid of a newcomer who was already hopelessly lost, but the ratio was about 25 or 30 novices for every veteran."

"Bully Lang of JG 54 (Green Hearts) went that way. In September, 1944, near St. Trond, during a battle with Thunderbolts, the 35 year old ex-Lufthansa pilot had the hydraulics of his Fw 190 shot out at low altitude. His gear came down, drastically cutting his speed and maneuverability, and he was done. Major Lang had gone to the aid of two young pilots, driving the P-47s off their backs."

Bomber Pilots

"With the critical lack of fuel, our bomber command virtually closed down, and in the early fall of 1944, we began getting another type replacement, ex-bomber, dive bomber and transport pilots. They were far more experienced certainly, but in many ways they were at a tremendous disadvantage too. Most of them didn't know how to shoot, couldn't make an attack, and didn't know how to take evasive action though their life depended on it. I've seen some with a fighter on their tail. They knew it, yet they would go into a gentle standard turn to try and shake the enemy, as though they were still flying bombers. You can imagine how long they lasted. They didn't seem to realize that in a fighter, a gentle turn is suicide. The only advantage they had was in lots of flying time and the fact they could fly instruments and navigate quite well."

"Many times, replacement pilots would come into a squadron in the evening, get a training flight the next morning and then go on a mission against the bombers and not come back that afternoon. There was simply nothing we could do about it."

"In late 1943 and early 1944, when the bomber formations went up without escorting fighters we hit them pretty hard. Then the P-51s and 47s began to escort them all the time; but would stay close to the bombers. This wasn't so bad, because when you broke away from your attacks they wouldn't follow you very far. Later on though, they got smart. They went hunting for us. There were fighters all over. You were likely to encounter them almost everywhere. Particularly after the invasion, they were around all the time. You had to be very careful and watchful or they would bounce you and shoot up a few planes from the formation before you knew they were there. This was particularly bad at low altitude because we couldn't see them as readily as we could higher up."

"We lost a great many inexperienced pilots this way. As long as they were with our formation they would do fairly well, but the minute they became separated, they'd just fly around aimlessly, trying to think what to do next, and pretty soon a P-47 or P-51 would come up on them and blow them from the sky."

Summer The Worst

"The longer hours of daylight in the summer and fall of 1944 and spring of '45 were the worst. After the invasion, we didn't have just the bombers to worry about. The fighters were roaming all over and we were likely to be scrambled at any time. We were on alert from before dawn to after dark, every day the weather was flyable and this can get very tiresome whether you fly or not. When we flew that summer, six sorties per day was not unusual."

"Fortunately, in 1945 I went to Me 262 school and it was a good rest. We flew Me 110s for a few hours as a refresher on multi-engines before checking out in the 262. The 110 is one aircraft I'm certainly thankful I didn't have to fly in combat or I wouldn't be here now talking to you. I really disliked it. It was underpowered, slow and took the strength of Hercules to fly, because it was so heavy on the controls."

"It was almost impossible to do any fast maneuvering with it because of the lead-like stick and rudder. Its reaction to control movement was quite good, but you simply couldn't move the damn things fast enough. It was like pushing furniture. Apparently it was capable of taking quite a bit of punishment because it was built very well. Certainly it needed to be, because the 110 didn't have a chance against any single engine fighter with even average maneuverability. They were wise to remove it from day combat as soon as they could and convert it to night fighting, where it acquitted itself quite well against the R.A.F. bombers."

"At the 262 school, we spent considerable time in mockups learning cockpit layout and attending classes on flying the airplane. Particular stress was laid to the operation of the engines, since they were quite critical. I was at this school for eight weeks and discovered all the peculiarities of flying a jet, such as no torque; slow acceleration and deceleration and the requirement for anticipating the throttle movements well in advance, when at low power settings."

"On the day I actually flew the aircraft for the first time, I was briefed, then started the engines and taxied out for take off while they coached me by radio. The first takeoff was quite an experience because of the slow acceleration and no torque. I thought it was never going to get off the ground. I had used up most of the runway when it finally lifted off and I breathed a sigh of relief."

"I flew around for 15 or 20 minutes getting the feel of the aircraft, then came in for my first landing. Very cautiously, I might add. My final approach pattern was very long and straight. Again, being coached from the ground by radio, I came straight in, gradually losing altitude and holding reduced power all the way. I set it up to be over the end of the runway just before I touched down. To go around required a decision long before you touched down, because the throttle had to be moved very slowly and acceleration was very poor at that speed and configuration."

"After completing the school, I telephoned General Adolf Galland and told him I was through school and asked to join his unit, JV-44."

His reply was simple: "Sure, and bring a jet along."

"In combat, the Me 262 called for a different technique than the 109, the controls were extremely heavy at 550-600 miles per hour and dogfighting was not possible. On the bombers we would come in well spaced, to cut down the defensive fire's concentration, in a long curved attack, fire bursts from our four 30mm cannon and then pull up and away into position for another attack. Normally, with a 109 or 190, getting back into position for a second attack was a time consuming thing, but with the 262 and its vastly superior speed over the bombers, it was no problem at all. Within a minute or two we were back in position again. This was crucial, because we had very limited endurance with the 262. Normally, we could expect 1:10 or 1:15 flying time but if we engaged in combat, the most we could count on was 50 to 55 minutes."

Speed Advantage

"Usually, to get at the bombers, we had to break through the escorting fighter formations, but with our tremendous speed advantage this wasn't difficult. We just had to be careful they didn't get into position above and dive on us before we saw them. I believe this was the way Galland and a few others were shot down. As long as we saw them, they posed few problems, because we could get away from them so quickly. Even with one engine out, we were generally faster than they were. I had an engine flame out once and still ran away from a flight of P-51s without any trouble. A slight dive and they couldn't catch me and soon fell behind."

"One of the most important criteria dictating our tactics with the 262, one which limited our attacks on the bombers to a long curving high speed attack, was the tremendous strength it took to move the controls at high speed. The stick was extra long for added leverage, but we had no aileron boost and at 550-650 miles per hour, moving the controls was like bending an iron bar. Dogfighting was simply impossible at these speeds so we just used our superior velocity to make a long curving attack, since any Allied fighter could turn inside of us."

"The speed of the Me 262 was critical at the high end because of yaw or snake, caused by compressibility. The minute it started it was imperative to throttle back and lose a little speed. This stopped the yaw very quickly and as long as we knew about it, we could overcome it."

"Between the top engine rpm of 7800 and 6000 rpm, the throttle could be moved fairly quickly, much like that in a conventional fighter, but below 6000 rpm we had to be very careful and move the throttle slowly, or we would encounter compressor stall and the engine would quit."

Landing Critical

"This tendency of the engine to quit with a movement of the throttle at low rpm and especially at low speed made the approach to landing critical and we were very vulnerable here. We kept some Fw 190s at the field to patrol it when we were landing just because of this problem, but we never had any difficulty with fighters following us home. Some of the other units did, such as *Kommando Nowotny*, but never JV-44."

"A word is in order here about our bases during the last six months of the war. From the fall of 1944 until the very end, we were so outnumbered by Allied fighters and continually subjected to strafing and bombing attacks, that many units simply disintegrated. Fuel could not be stored in large quantities, replacement depot parks disappeared, the planes being flown directly from the factory to the front, and even repair and test facilities had to be dissassembled and scattered to remove them as likely targets. The *Ami Jabos* (American fighter bombers) were on us, whenever a so-called target of opportunity presented itself. Therefore, we could only concentrate during periods of bad weather. As a result, we took to using the *autobahn* system, as a long, improvised runway."

"In many respects this was an improvement over our regular bases. It was long, its concrete strips were numerous and, during the day, two to three fighters could be hidden under its many underpasses. Furthermore, the surrounding woods made for ideal field maintenance. They usually lined the *autobahn* for miles and we soon found ourselves sharing these woodland hideouts with nightfighters and even large four engined bombers such as the Fw 200 Condor."

"Since normal civilian automobile traffic had long since ended, the highways were virtually empty. Ammunition, fuel and supplies could be quickly brought to us from nearby towns along the excellent network and for inexperienced pilots, especially, the *autobahns* proved particularly handy. They could be seen for miles from the air, they were mainly long straight roadbeds and there were enough of them throughout Germany to insure that a pilot running low on fuel or, with a damaged aircraft, could find a safe, if temporary, haven."

"During the last months of the war morale became a serious problem. But although everyone knew defeat was coming, they kept working, pilots and ground crewman alike. The Americans were particularly keen to cripple the few remaining jet bases and were out in packs hunting for us. Our fields and concrete runways were pitted by their bombs and their fighters returned again and again to strafe our remaining planes. Jet fuel was desperately short and the majority of our brand new aircraft were destroyed while awaiting fuel or transportation to a combat base."

"The Americans even went after our pilots, shooting at them in their parachutes or after they had reached the ground. Take off and landings across plowed up runways, hastily patched together by relays of exhausted ground crew workers, were even more difficult than the missions and above us, hordes of American fighters were out on constant patrol."

From its last base at Reim, JV-44 made one final sortie in strength against a huge force of 1,300 B-17s from the 1st and 3rd Divisions. A total of 50 Me 262s were brought together in an attempt to deal one last crippling blow at the bomber stream which had decimated Germany. Over Oranienburg, they struck at the first formations, attacking from the rear, in pairs, singling out those stragglers who had strayed from the main body. JV-44 claimed 25 kills with their 5cm R4M rockets, but the 8th Air Force reported the loss of only ten aircraft while claiming an unrealistic 15 jets shot down."

Actually during the last months of the war, German losses were difficult to gauge. Many records branches had been either overrun or destroyed. In the case of the jet squadrons, a majority of their aircraft were shot up on the ground or shot down while in the landing pattern, where they were most vulnerable."

While the fighter squadrons in the east remained more or less intact, and continued to fly and fight as they had for two years, operating from improvised bases, those in the west became disoriented. Many of the Luftwaffe's best pilots had transferred to jet aircraft, responding to the call, 'for great guns,' as Johannes Steinhoff put it. Before they went under they wanted one final chance at air superiority, even if only for a limited time, and the Me 262 provided that opportunity. The remainder of German pilots, many of them newcomers, and all of them flying piston-engined aircraft, found themselves in units whose strength had been drastically cut. Depleted handfulls of 15 aircraft were put up by the pitiful remnants of once mighty groups. In some areas, fighter wings were not much bigger than squadrons had once been. Shorn of their veterans these units were forced to go up against impossible odds. They no longer flew from permanent stations, or slept in comfortable barracks. The last months in the west were beginning to resemble the spartan living conditions which had predominated in the east from the beginning.

—Joseph V. Mizrahi

Chapter 5
Defending The
Reich Against The Russians

Note: Adolf Hitler's decision to open a military campaign against the Soviet Union, in the spring of 1941, was his most dangerous gamble of World War II and set the stage for Germany's greatest catastrophe.

Why did Hitler reach this decision? In Hitler's eyes, the Soviet Union had always been the ideological enemy which, because of its extortionist policies, would sooner or later attack Germany from the rear. The steady expansion of Soviet power and the suspicious actions of Russian representatives during the many political, military and economic conferences with Germany after 1939 strengthened his belief in the inevitability of war with the Soviet Union. In the conduct of its war against the West, Germany had a considerable dependence upon raw materials imported from Russia, and the continuance of this supply was, in great part, dependent on the "good will" of the Soviet Union. Militarily, Russia had been active, seizing the Baltic States, Bessarabia and Bucovina and part of Finland, and increasing its western frontier forces.

After considerable staff planning, backed by Hitler's belief that the war in the East could be concluded in three of four months, the directives and orders for Operation BARBAROSSA were issued in January 1941. The attack on Russia was to be launched in early May, but in the meantime the German forces had to be sent into the Balkans, to secure their southern flank, following the March 27, 1941 coup d'etat in Yugoslavia. The sweep through the Balkans delayed BARBAROSSA five weeks. A very late thaw in Russia further held back the start of the attack so that when it did begin it was almost two months late, a delay that was perhaps decisive.

At 0330 hours on 22 June 1941, the surprise attack against the Soviet Union began. Opposing about 8,000 Russian military aircraft, the Luftwaffe haf deployed some 2,000 of its own combat aircraft (leaving 190 for home defense, 370 in the Mediterranean, 660 in the West and 120 in Norway). The Fourth Air Fleet, supporting Army Group South, had 600 combat aircraft—360 medium and light bombers, 210 fighters and 30 long range reconaissance planes, plus 60 transports and 30 liaison planes.

Assigned to Army Group Center were some 910 combat planes of the Second Air Fleet—240 medium and light bombers, 250 dive bombers, 270 single engine and 60 twin engine fighters, 60 ground attack planes and 30 long range recon planes, plus 60 transports and 30 liaison planes. The

First Air Fleet supported Army Group North with about 430 aircraft—270 medium or light bombers, 110 fighters and 50 long range recon planes, plus 30 transports and 20 liaison planes. On the extreme left of the German front was Army Command Far North, Supported by the Fifth Air Fleet with 10 medium bombers, 30 dive bombers, 10 fighters and 10 long range recon planes.

Outnumbered some four to one, the Luftwaffe had an abundance of high quality aircraft and favorable weather as it launched continuous high and low level air attack early on 22 June with 637 dive and conventional bombers and 231 fighters. This first attack wave struck 31 Soviet airfields near the border, 3 staff billets, 2 barracks, 2 artillary positions, a bunker system and an oil depot. Only two Luftwaffe planes were missing. By the end of the day, no les than 1,800 Russian planes had been destroyed on the ground and in the air. By the end of one week, Hermann Goering, Marshall of the Luftwaffe, announced 4,990 Russian planes destroyed against a loss of 179 Luftwaffe aircraft.

So was near total air superiority quickly won. By 25 June, the Luftwaffe's second mission had begun, the full support of German ground operations. Sorties against Soviet air forces and their ground installations were subsequently flow only occasionally, and only when the steadily increasing Russian air activity became too bothersome for the German ground forces or caused them unbearable losses. Holding to such a policy gave the almost totally destroyed Russian Air Force a chance to regroup, reequip and reenter the battle by winter, this time with significant effect.

By the winter of 1941, the Germans had advanced greatly but were mired down before Moscow and Leningrad in the center and north and just beyond Kharkov in the south. The short campaign was not to be, but, as a few examples will show, the Luftwaffe had more than done its job.

On 9 July, units of JG 3 (fighter wing 3 with Me 109s), commanded by Major Guenther Luetzow, took to the air when their airfield was attacked by 27 Russian bombers and shot down the entire force in 15 minutes without loss. Between 22 June and 26 July, SKG 210 (fast bomber wing 210 with Me 110s) flew 1,574 sorties, destroyed 92 enemy planes in the air and 823 on the ground, and destroyed or put out of action 165 tanks, 2,136 motor vehicles, 194 cannon, 52 trains and 60 locomotives. From 22 June through 31 July, ZG 26 (long range fighter wing 26 with Me 110s) destroyed 620 Soviet aircraft in aerial combat and low level attacks.

By 17 August, heavy fighting had reduced the Fourth Air Fleet's V Air Corps to 44 fighters (from 90), but the I and II Gruppen of JG 3 and the III Gruppe of JG 52 downed 33 enemy planes that day, including 29 bombers, and destroyed 3 on the ground. On the 30th of August, JG 3 shot down its 1000th Russian plane. An attack on an airfield 17 miles SW of Leningrad on 19 August saw ZG 26 set 30 fighters on fire, destroy 15 more and shoot down 3, thus increasing its total claims to 191 in the air and 663 on the ground. The 8th of September saw JG 51 of the Second Air Fleet score its 2001st air victory, and by 10 September its Russian front claims were 1,357 enemy aircraft in the air and 298 on the ground, plus 142 tanks and armored cars, 34 locomotives, 432 trucks and 75 miscellaneous vehicles in 354 strafing attacks.

The Fourth Air Fleet's, IV Air Corps, JG 77, commanded by Major Gotthardt Handrick, scored its 800th aerial victory on October 20th. From

22 June through 12 November, General der Flieger Bruno Loerzer announced, the flying units of the II Air Corps, Second Air Fleet, had flown over 40,000 day and night sorties, shot down 2,169 Soviet planes and destroyed 1,657 on the ground, probably destroyed 281 more and damaged 811. It also destroyed 789 tanks, 614 artillery pieces, 14,339 vehicles, 159 trains and 304 locomotives. □

The geography of Russia, its lack of a modern system of communications, its primitive, almost medieval village and town structure, had almost as great an impact on the air war between Germany and the Soviet Union, as the men and material engaged. With the exception of the main highway from Poland to Moscow, no modern road networks existed. The approaches to large cities such as Leningrad and Kharkov included asphalt highways, but these were only one lane each way and soon petered out a few miles beyond the city's environs. Ninety percent of Russia's villages and towns between the great cities had no electricity. At night, everything was black. There were no beacons, no reference points, no radio directional fixes, no landmarks. When the sun went down, the war in the air ceased.

Few Airfields

As the Luftwaffe moved east, it found few, if any, enemy airfields to occupy. Even municipal airports in cities such as Minsk, Kiev, Orel, all of them large in terms of population, possessed but rudimentary flying fields. Military airdromes which had fallen during the first week of the campaign, were of little use to the Luftwaffe, since they were soon left behind the quickly advancing front. The subsequent capture of succeding Soviet bases were of similar value, In the main these consisted of a large cleared area and a few temporary buildings. There were no hangars, no storage facilities, no water supply more sophisticated than a nearby river or stream. In effect, the Russians had given up very little. Anything of value was usually destroyed and Luftwaffe engineers soon discovered that they would be better off starting from scratch, than attempting to rebuild former Russian installations.

Because these Red Air Force fields had so little to offer, German pilots frequently found themselves quartered in schools, post offices and collective farm buildings, anything substantial enough to withstand the rigors of a Russian winter. In most cases, these buildings had no electricity and were, instead, illuminated by gaslight or candles. Running water was a luxury, indoor plumbing a myth of the future. Living in these off-base, makeshift quarters, German pilots traveled to their nearby fields by wagon, horseback, jeep and, in winter, by improvised snowplows which consisted of captured ammunition carriers or half-tracks to which large, spade-shaped iron wedges had been attached. In winter, units would be snowed in for weeks at a time. The aircraft would be covered with tarpaulins and left beneath 20 to 30 ft. of piled up snow. There was not way to get to the planes. All road traffic was impossible. Under such conditions, the fighting simply stopped. Neither side could move and stalemate settled over the silent white steppe.

With the coming of spring, after the first thaw, which left roads and fields a quagmire, the fighting resumed. Summer was a fly infested nightmare of seemingly endless, insufferably humid days. Then, in the fall, after the dried up earth had turned to dust, spinning off the brown plains like desert sand storms, the air grew crisp and sharp with the coming of winter and the cycle repeated itself. Summers were short and hot, winters long and overpowering. During the brief spring and fall, the air war shook off its torpor. In summer it raged unabated, culminating in giant autumnal battles where aircraft fell like the leaves of the dark brooding forests. Between April and November, with the exception of strategic bombing in the west, the air combat in the east had nothing to equal it for savagery and non-stop fury.

Because so many German aces scored the bulk of their victories on the Eastern Front, it has been accepted as fact, in too many quarters, that victories in the east were gained easily. This is not true.

Two Part Conflict

The air war over Russia was really a two part conflict. The first lasted two years and ended in the summer of 1943. The second began that same summer and continued to the gates of Berlin two years later. During the first two years of fighting the Russian air force was a huge, but unwieldy arm. Its aircraft were crude by western standards, many were obsolete and the majority were devoid of auxiliary systems such as hydraulic landing gear, bullet proof windshielding, oxygen, gun heaters and even gunsights. Erich Hartmann recalls the first Russian aircraft he saw had sights which consisted of a handpainted circle on the windshield.

Others, such as Gerhard Barkhorn (WW II's second leading ace with 301 victories), remembers the early Russian pilots as a mob of amateurs, whose overall inadequacies were emphasized by the performance of the occasional professional one encountered within their ranks. They flew in massed formations reminiscent of the First World War, and invariably at low altitude. Consequently they were usually at a height disadvantage and although they outnumbered Luftwaffe pilots five to one, their lack of training and cumbersome tactics, gave the advantage to the Germans. Barkhorn recalls that "many of them were never taught to clear their tails. They never looked around in the cockpit and it was relatively easy to approach a flight of them and score several kills before they knew what was happening."

A great deal of the Russian's ineptitude during the first two years of fighting was due to the fact that their air force was tied completely to their ground forces. Even as the war progressed and Russian pilots and equipment improved, they never acted as an independent arm. Their bomber force was notorious for its lack of strategic punch and the inability of its crews to navigate to, and hit, distant targets. During WW II, the Russian air force was primarily a tactical arm and the only impressive bomber aircraft developed by it were close support strike machines, the 11-2 Stormavik and the Petlyakov Pe-2.

Used offensively as flying artillery—to soften up key positions for tank assaults, as well as defensively—to stop armored counterattacks, both these aircraft were employed on all sectors of the front. In many ways their utilization was similar to that favored by the Germans. For the Luftwaffe's bomber force was also tactically oriented. Like that of the Soviets' it was capable of only a limited strategic role. Since the main combat arena was close to the front line, on offense, the bombers preceded the massed pincer encirclements; on defense, they plugged gaps in the anti-tank walls.

Because of this tactical aspect, aerial combat took place down on the deck where dive bombers and cannon, or rocket-armed strafers operate best. Since the bombers were low, their escorting fighters were not far above them and thus, the intercepting German fighters were also forced down low in order to break up the massive Soviet air armadas.

Given this set of critieria, combat flying on the eastern front took on the quality of a lethal, low level fly-by, a kind of ground hugging melee in which streams of attack planes were constantly being broken into by flights of interceptors. In this type of aerial battle, the barrage of fire from the ground installations was incredibly deadly. Most of the flying took place below 6,000 ft., a good deal of it under 2,000 ft. Viewed from a distance, an air battle here, as one German pilot described it, "was more like a black, pulsating mass of insects boiling up over a huge grass fire."

For the trained Luftwaffe pilot, these engagements offered the chance to score victories in bunches. An accomplished "expert" and his wingman could hit the main body of Russian attack bombers, score four or five kills and be gone, before their escorts could counterattack.

That they did so, and often, is clearly obvious when one tallies the large number of attack planes among their victims, (perhaps 50 percent.) Nevertheless, as the war progressed, this kind of flying proved exhausting. Always outnumbered, the odds grew longer against the Luftwaffe, as the fighting drew out. Stationed close to the front, it was not unusual for a Luftwaffe fighter pilot to fly between five and seven sorties in a 24 hour period, especially in the summer when the long North European day dawns at four in the morning and does not end until dusk at eleven. Under such conditions, the enemy was always encountered. The air above the tank battlefield was alive with planes and if this situation provided an unprecedented opportunity to becoming an ace many times over, it was also conducive to quickly terminating one's career.

The battle was incessant, the pressure to join combat unrelenting. The Germans were invariably short handed and if the Russians were not the most sophisticated of antagonists, there were so many of them that, as Erich Hartmann puts it, "30 of us against 300 of them, usually evened things out."

Improved Training and Aircraft

After 1943, however, a dramatic shift took place. The Russians were no longer flying obsolete aircraft. Their pilot training improved markedly and although the presence of the tactical bomber continued to dictate the pace and position of the air battle, it was now much more difficult to get to them. The Guard Regiments which often shepherded the bombers were competent professionals; their planes were faster and better armed. Many were lend-lease types provided by the western allies . . . nearly 9,000 flighters alone (Fig. 5-1). In practically every instance, the Germans were on the defensive and if the Luftwaffe numbered cadres of outstanding pilots among its ranks, those ranks were thinning, while those of the enemy continued to swell.

The war in the East, particularly, proved how short the Luftwaffe was of specialist aircraft. There, its two principal fighters, the Me 109 and the Fw 190, were forced to carry the brunt of both fighter and fighter-escort operations, as well as fighter/

Fig. 5-1. The United States supplied 2,019 Curtiss P-40s to Russia during WW-II, along with a large number of other aircraft. In the hands of a skilled pilot, the P-40 Warhawk was a match for the Me 109 below 15,000 ft (the Warhawk had no supercharger for high altitude operation); but man-for-man the Soviet pilots were no match for the Germans.

bomber and attack missions, even though both had been designed as interceptors from the outset.

For the Me 109 the metamorphosis was critical. With heavy armament and the added weight, in its G model, the aircraft had no range (Fig. 5-2). Even during the close-in fighting typified by the Eastern Front, drop tanks were invariably necessary. When pressed into service as a fighter bomber or Jabo, the 109 had to be flown, literally, from immediately behind the front line. If asked to perform as an interceptor, its wing guns had to be deleted to provide an acceptable standard of maneuverability. Added horsepower was only a partial answer, as the airframe, then nearly a decade old, had been stretched to where it offered improvements of dubious value. The critical point in the 109's development had been reached in the spring of 1941 when the F model was introduced (Fig. 5-3). A clean, esthetically pleasing flying machine, it carried none of the armament bumps and drag producers of later models and had eliminated many of the wedge-shaped characteristics of the earlier 109E's chunkier silhouette (Fig. 5-4). But with only a single nose cannon and a pair of rifle caliber machine guns, it did not have the firepower of the E. Veterans like Moelders and Udet preferred it that way. The F climbed well, turned tightly and was the last classic Messerschmitt dogfighter. This was fine, if one were an experienced ace, but Adolf Galland and Walter Oesau clearly saw that as the war progressed the number of veteran marksmen would dwindle, while the ranks of raw recruits, many of them the product of accelerated flying school crash programs, would swell. These new pilots would know very little of unerring marksmanship. The would have their hands full just flying the airplane. The would invariably be outnumbered, and Galland and Oesau didn't want them to be outgunned, too. They demanded that the new 109s carry more firepower, at the expense of performance, and Oesau went so far as to refuse to fly the 109F for several months, even though his wing, JG 1 had already re-equipped with it.

In the end, gunpower won out over performance, and many a Luftwaffe pilot, veteran and novice alike, paid the price when his fighter could not take him out of harm's way, or was unable to execute the rough maneuver needed to save his life.

Combat for Luftwaffe aces on the Eastern Front was similar to the oft-told dilemma of the Dutch boy with his finger in the dike. The only difference being that there were more leaks in the structure than there were fighters on hand. A crack wing such as JG 52 with its 120 to 1 aircraft could probably achieve air superiority over any given sector of front. By spreading its groups thin, it could possibly maintain tenuous control over portions of adjacent sectors, but what could one wing do when confronted by ten and,

Fig. 5-2. Early Me 109Gs were produced with two 7.9-mm cowl guns. Altogether, 30,480 Me 109s were built. The Luftwaffe lost a total of 70,030 airmen killed, 1939-1944. The US Strategic Bombing Survey lists a total of 79,265 American and 79,281 British airmen lost in action for the entire war. Russian losses are unavailable to Free World researchers.

Fig. 5-3. An Me 109F of JG 54 on a makeshift airfield in Russia.

sometimes twenty to one odds, not only on a single sector, but on half a dozen?

This then was the air war in the East. After 1943 the Germans were continually on the defensive against an enemy who grew stronger and more capable. Those pilots who survived the ever growing disparity of numbers and continued to operate on the narrowing margin for error, achieved tremendous victory scores. Those who didn't were quickly eliminated, leaving what, in effect, became a nucleus of super aces. Their proficiency could not be matched anywhere, simply because nowhere else had pilots operated for so long, under such adverse conditions and survived.

For those who tend to downgrade the scores of men like Erich Hartmann, Gerhard Barkhorn, Wilhelm Batz and Walter Wolfrum, because they achieved nearly all their scores in the east, it should be remembered that Hartmann did not score his first victory until 1943 when the day of "easy" victories was already over. Gerhard Barkhorn was shot down nine times, Hartmann sixteen, and both had memorable duels with Russian pilots, long after they had become aces, pilots who either bested them or fought them to a draw. Some of the greatest Luftwaffe pilots were killed in the east, men like Otto Kittel and Anton Hafner, who scored over 470 victories between them. If such facts do not testify to the rigors of combat in the east, one had only to look at the records of two Russian Aces, Ivan Kojedub with 62 victories and Alexander Pokryshin with 59. No ace among the French, British or Americans scored more than 38 victories against German flown aircraft.

Spector of Capture

Perhaps the greatest fear German pilots on the eastern front lived with was the constant spector of capture by the Russians. Early in the war, the Russians let it be known that they would treat any German pilots who fell into their hands as war criminals. Posters and leaflets were distributed which made it clear, in no uncertain terms, what fate would befall any Luftwaffe pilots who fell into their hands. Torture, pure and simple, headed the list of handbills which were periodically dropped over German bases. This threat, combined with the awesome vastness of Russia itself, an endless bog of mud in spring, an empty, sun-scorched plain in summer and a waste of howling cold in winter, caused some men to crack. Nobody liked to fly too far behind the Russian lines, but this could not be avoided, even if most air battles took place right above the front. Reconnaissance patrols were frequent and everyone had to go on them. Fear of capture became so ingrained among German pilots, particularly well known aces for whom the Russians reserved particularly gruesome epithets in their circulars, that one Hans Strelow, a Knights Cross winner from JG 51 (Molders) with 68 victories, shot himself rather than be taken prisoner, in May, 1942.

Strelow was a squadron leader at the time and as the war progressed, becoming a vendetta on both sides, his terror of capture had grown. Russian strength also grew. Despite having had entire fleets wiped out during the first months of *Barbarossa* in 1941, the Soviets had bounced back with more planes, better machines and improved pilots. Even though huge scores had been run up by the pilots of the Luftwaffe, including occasions where veterans like Major Emil "Bully" Lang of JG 54 (Green Hearts) shot down an incredible 72 aircraft in only three weeks, eighteen in one day, an all time record for any fighter pilot, survival was becoming more difficult. The Russians lost nearly 80,000 aircraft during WW II, many of them destroyed on the ground. Among them, three wings, JG 51, 52 and 54, destroyed more than 28,000 aircraft and still there was no end to the Russians. Their production

Fig. 5-4. An Me 109E-4 of JF 27 escorts a Stuka over Russia.

rate was nearly three times that of Germany's and in addition to the more than 130,000 combat aircraft they delivered between June 1941 and June 1945, they received another 15,000 aircraft from their Allies.

Outmanned at least five to one and often twenty to one, the German figher pilots faced odds far more critical than faced by the British during the Battle of Britian, and they did so for nearly four years.

In order to overcome both the strain and the enemy, German pilots became proficient at a great many things other than flying and air-to-air gunnery. Although revered and honored in Germany, they soon learned to become inconspicuous in Russia. The wreath and victory rudder markings so common in the west were quickly dispensed with in the east. All such ace markings usually disappeared, and with them went command and staff insignia. German aces flew incognito if possible and, in order to appear as ordinary pilots, wing and group leaders such as Wilhelm Batz and Guenther Rall changed their code leader names every few weeks. They never flew under their own names. During one stretch, Batz, flying under the code name *Rabitsky*, kept using it for too long. The Russians, under their own ace, Ivanov, soon learned that Batz, who flew a relatively unmarked 109G, was *Rabitsky*. They monitored his radio transmissions and set a trap for him.

Four Russian fighters including Ivanov, jumped him out of the sun while flying at 18,000 ft. They had a height advantage of nearly 3,000 ft. and when Batz half rolled and made a steep reverse, going back the way he had come, he was hit by eight more Russian fighters, coming up from below. Again he quickly reversed, diving again until the airspeed needle reached nearly 600 mph. The 109 vibrated like a truck on a washboard road. Despite his quick reactions, Batz had been hit badly. He managed to elude his pursuers, but when he landed, his aircraft simply collapsed. It was a total write off, the wings beginning to separate from the fuselage.

To understand how they were able to run up such incredible victory strings, when the top aces of the Western Allies scored no more than 40 kills, one has to remember that the Luftwaffe aces flew up to ten times as many sorties, and they usually met an enemy willing to engage. They never had to go far and the longer they flew, the more they learned. They discovered techniques, and devices few other fighter pilots, with the exception of the Japanese, could relate to, simply because they did it so often. Their tours were never cut short to sell war bonds. Only death retired them, and so they amassed a unique type of experience that no training school could ever teach. They truly became expert in their grim business and eventually flew into a realm of proficiency unknown and unknowable to others. Pressure will always promote performance and in the case of the Luftwaffe's aces, unrelenting pressure gave rise to truly amazing exploits . . . it also caused the death of many pilots who had nothing more to give.

In concluding this summary of the air war on the eastern front one should remember that although the majority of Russian pilots were not as skilled as their western counterparts, they were tough, pugnacious and incredibly brave. They had no compunctions about ramming an opponent and, if flying against them was something akin to, "shooting against a barn door," as Hans Phillip described it, "where one did not need to know how to fly, but only shoot," there were still enough good Russian pilots in the opposing mass to kill you.

Because they were always outnumbered, because their living conditions were the most primitive by far, even worse than that of Africa, those German fighter pilots who survived the war in the east are a very special breed. Their accomplishments cannot be overlooked or played down.

Erich Hartmann

Of all Luftwaffe fighter aces, Erich Hartmann was the acknowledged king. In an exchange of correspondence during the summer of 1968, WW II's highest scoring ace (352 victories) made available the following information.

Between the end of 1942 and May, 1945, Hartmann flew 1,425 combat missions. He engaged the enemy during 800 of them and averaged approximately two aircraft shot down every fifth time he found and fired at the enemy. Viewed in that perspective, his incredible victory string does not appear unbelievable. What is astounding is how he managed to survive the war. For in addition to encountering vast numbers of enemy aircraft while flying literally round-the-clock missions, he was forced to face some of the most brutal and concentrated ground fire of the war.

Already an accomplished glider pilot at 17 when war broke out, Hartmann volunteered for air cadet training in October, 1940, but he was not sent to the front for another two years. Posted to the 7th Staffel of III/JG 52, he arrived at Soldatskaia, in the Caucasus, on October 2, 1942. The brand new lieutenant-pilot's first combat aircraft was the 109G-6, he was 20 years old.

His first month at the front, Hartmann was shot down twice, crashlanding both times. The second crash resulted in a brain concussion and he was hospitalized. He was also disillusioned. His combat career had not begun on a promising note, and he requested a transfer to the infantry. Fortunately for him, the commander of JG 52, Hermann Graf, the first ace to score 200 victories, did not share Hartmann's view of his abilities. When he was released from the hospital, in January, 1943, Hartmann was swiftly returned to combat and almost immediately shot down his first aircraft, a cannon-armed Yak 9.

What were the qualities that made Hartmann so deadly? Words are a poor substitute for performance but the following factors stand out.

1. A complete familiarity with his aircraft.
2. A thorough knowledge of his and his enemy's abilities.
3. An outstanding marksman.

Ask any fighter pilot about his career and he will invariably tell you that a great measure of his success depended on luck. Hartmann himself, attributes his success to various factors. "Good fortune and determination had a lot to do with it," he says, "as well as the experience which was shared with me by my first teachers at the front."

During an interview conducted in the summer of 1968, Hartmann commented on the ingredients necessary for surviving as a fighter pilot. "You must understand and analyze the various situations you may find yourself in, before they arise. Then you must learn how to exploit them. One of my first leaders and teachers was Warrant Officer Rossmann. I began my career with the 7th Staffel of III/JG 52 flying his wing. He taught me discipline combat flying, as opposed to merely piloting the aircraft. A brilliant tactician, he had a feel for every situation and a countermeasure to cope with it. Flying with Rossmann I learned never to separate from my leader, to always cover him and protect him during the attack, and never to lose my orientation. From him I also learned how to protect and break-in my own wingman. Of all the accomplishments I may have achieved during the war, I am proudest of the fact that I never lost a wingman. No kill was ever worth the life of your comrade, many of whom were young and inexperienced boys, particularly during the later stages of the war. In my units, any pilot who lost a wingman through negligence, had to give up his position and fly wing instead.

"Once I learned how to quickly recognize tactical situations, I was then able to exploit them. From Warrant Officer Alfred Grislawski (later promoted to Captain—133 victories) I learned to go all out, once I had chosen my method of attack. Hesitation is the nemesis of a fighter pilot. Once the decision has been reached on how and when to engage the enemy, action must follow immediately. This is why it is so necessary to recognize a tactical situation as it develops, right now. It was Grislawsky who showed me the weakness in the I1-2 Stormavik, the vulnerable oil cooler, beneath its fuselage. Shooting at it anywhere else was usually a waste of ammunition.

"From Warrant Officer Hans Dammers (later promoted to lieutenant—113 victories) and Captain Walter Krupinski (197 victories) I learned how to shoot. Both lent an air of recklessness, but controlled recklessness, to my style and showed me how to score hits.

The Closer the Better

"The key to their approach was simple: Get as close to the enemy as possible. Your windscreen had to be black with image . . . the closer the better. In that position you could not miss and this was the essence of my attack. The farther away you are from the enemy, the more chance your bullets have of missing the target, the less their impact. When you are close, and I mean really close, every shot hits home. The enemy absorbs it all. It doesn't matter what your angle on him is, or what position you are firing from. It doesn't matter what he does. When you are that close, evasion is useless and too late. It matters not how good a pilot he is. All his skill is negated, your guns hit him and he goes down.

"But for this kind of flying, you have to know your aircraft. You can't get jittery, even when you feel you are getting too close. Because the fact is, you cannot get too close. Even 100 yards from the other machine is not close enough. At that stage, fearing a mid air collision, the inexperienced pilot will break away, and that is when he will be shot down, but the veteran will continue to bore in, and the enemy will go down. At times, I have gotten so close, as near as 15 yards, that debris from the explosion of the other aircraft has forced me down. Yet despite being shot down 16 times, I was never wounded.

"Closing the enemy always insured kills, usually with little expenditure of ammunition and, for a fighter pilot, conserving ammunition gets high priority. Wasting it is foolish. You may need it later on, and shooting from long range is a guaranteed waste. At close range, the shortest of split second bursts will get the job done, because, at that range, all are going into the target. Your projectiles are also striking with much more power, and they are also concentrating in a much smaller area. Firing from far off disperses your strikes. Even if the target is hit, that will not guarantee it going down. The other plane will usually absorb the strikes. Your hits are difficult to see and you will be forced to shoot three and four times as much ammunition in order to get even 25 percent of the hits you can record from closer in. On the other hand, when you are in close, pieces begin to fly off the target immediately. You know you are hitting from the first. You can see it, and then the machine explodes.

"If I had to summarize all this, I would say that in close, there is no guesswork. If you fly in there, you know you will score. Thus the key to getting in close and hitting the enemy is based on your method of attack and this, in turn, should always be based on the following. Once committed to an attack, fly in at full speed. After scoring crippling or disabling hits, I would clear myself and then repeat the process. I never pursued an enemy, once he had eluded me. Better to break off and set up again for a new assault. I always began my attacks from strength, if possible, my ideal flying height being 22,000 ft. because at that altitude I could best utilize the performance of my aircraft.

"In combat flying, fancy, precision aerobatic work is really not of much use. Instead, it is the rough maneuver which succeeds. When I was fourteen I had already gotten my gliding certificate. At 16 I had my C certificate. But although the years of soaring were to stand me in good stead throughout my flying career, particularly in judging distances and getting the "feel" of flying, I had to unlearn a great deal to fly combat and survive. Aerobatics are useful for giving one confidence in himself and his aircraft, in different regimes of flight. They are useful for the experience they provide in maintaining one's orientation, but precision aerobatics will get you killed in combat. Combat flying is based on the slashing attack and the rough maneuver. The whole idea is not to get into a situation where you must rely on 'fancy flying' to escape. Rather the idea is to attack to your best advantage and get in so close that no maneuver can shake you off. Closing the range is the great equalizer. When your enemy turns your windshield black with his fuselage, every trick maneuver he ever learned is just so much textbook academia.

"I always flew the Messerschmidt 109 begining with the G-6 and ending with the K-16, and although I trained on the Me 262 jet,

I never flew it in combat.

"The G model had far more power than the F, but the gain was more than offset by heavier armament. It had a fine rate of climb and handled well in all flight regimes. In the east, the most dangerous fighter was the Yak 9 with a 37mm engine-mounted cannon (Yak-9T). It could out-turn any opposing fighter and although rudimentary and even crude by western standards, it was very effective and dependable. It also had nearly twice the range of a 109."

Although Hartmann was a born hunter and invariably on the attack, he, too, was forced to fight at a disadvantage. An uncanny sixth sense which told him to beware, even when the sky around him appeared empty, saved his life on several occasions. Perhaps this was only super vision, prompted by an ever cautious distrust of "safe" areas. Whatever the reason, Hartmann was perpetually watchful and always alert, but he was only human, and when the victim of a sudden attack, he relied on a defense that was as simple and well thought out, in its own way, as his slashing offensive maneuvers.

"Pilots who liked to dogfight could do it their own way. I avoided it. I always attacked at full speed and I evaded a bounce in the same manner. When you were hit from above and behind, and your attacker held his fire until he was really close, you knew you were in with someone who had a great deal of experience. In that case, I would put my machine into a hard climbing turn, and turn into the enemy's pass. If he came in from below, I would also turn hard into the enemy and then go low. In most cases this maneuver spoils the attacker's aim and, more important, cuts short the time he has you under his guns. It breaks the sequence of the attack and gives you the opportunity to become the attacker.

Avoided Dogfights

"If taken by surprise, I would do one or the other automatically, depending on conditions. If I had time, and saw my attacker coming in, I would wait to see how close he would come before opening up. If he began firing at long range, I could always turn into him. If he held his fire, I got ready for a real battle. Even against good competition, you could always break away by using negative Gs. In a tight turning maneuver, the attacker must turn more tightly in order to pull lead on his quarry. For a split second, you pass under his nose and below his line of sight, as he tries to line his guns up ahead of you. It is precisely at that moment when he gets his gunnery angle on you, that you push the nose forward, kick bottom rudder and are gone. Your attacker cannot see you. He is intent on pulling lead and is turning in the opposite direction, in an ever tighter circle, even as you are diving and then turning the other way. As I said before, the use of negative G is a last ditch measure. Frankly, I tried everything possible never to be placed in such a position, because if your attacker had a good wingman, he could quickly pick up that maneuver. This is also why I avoided dogfights. They were long and drawn out affairs, requiring all your attention, allowing another opponent to jump you. They were the longest and most difficult method of getting a kill, the most expensive and the most dangerous."

In two and one half years, in which he engaged the enemy nearly 850 times, Hartmann was almost always the attacker, and his methods were so brilliant that although outnumbered and constantly singled out by the Soviets as *Karaya* One, his code name, he never suffered a scratch in combat. One of his last wingmen, the only one who was ever shot down, an ex bomber pilot, Major Guenther Capito, recalls the ace of aces. It was near the end of the war, and the 32 year old Capito, newly assigned as a fighter pilot, was having trouble squaring the image before him with the legend that had won not only the Knights Cross, but the swords, diamonds and oak leaves to go with it.

A peacetime professional pilot, Capito could not reconcile himself to the random, almost haphazzard routine which had become the norm at a frontline fighter unit. Its lack of discipline and casual disregard of military conduct was nearly scandalous and its lax group commander Hartmann was, *"a gangling baby-faced, sloppy young man. He wore a crushed cap pulled down tightly over a mass of matted, unmanageable hair. He slouched in his chair and talked with a maddeningly slow drawl. He was unkempt and appeared to have nothing to say, unless the talk turned to flying combat. Then he came alive."*

Although Hartmann tried to dissuade Capito from flying combat, telling him the war would be over soon, the older pilot kept urging his commander to allow him to fly his wing. After admonishing Capito to stay close and to forego slow standard bomber turns, Hartmann relented. In an air battle with Russian Airacobras, Capito neglected to follow his leader's instructions and was promptly shot down. He bailed out, but was picked up safely, Hartmann shooting down his attacker. Together they went over to the downed Russian's plane. The Soviet pilot was an ace, Capito had been his 26th victim. In 1,400 missions he was the only wingman Hartmann ever lost.

Joseph V. Mizrahi

Chapter 6
Combat Flying
the Messerschmitt 109

As early as November, 1939 an Me 109E-3 had fallen into Allied hands when its pilot became lost and landed it, intact, on the wrong side of the border. After undergoing comparison tests by the French Army of the Air, it was shipped to Boscombe Down, England for further evaluation. In general the British test pilots like the 109 (Fig. 6-1).

"Its direct fuel injection engine allows instantaneous acceleration. The aircraft's tail comes up quickly on take off and if allowed to fly itself off, the 109 is very smooth and breaks ground quickly. Climbing ability is exceptionally good, better than that of the Spitfire or Hurricane. At medium and low speeds, it rolls quickly and maneuvers well. Aileron and elevator controls are very responsive at speeds below 250 mph., but above 300 mph they became sluggish and above 400 mph. the ailerons lose 80% of their movement. Of the three major controls the rudder retains its ability longer, to move the aircraft precisely.

"In a dogfight the 109 performs well at speeds below 250 mph. Its controllability is exceptional. Ample stall warning is given in tight turns and if the stick is pulled back abruptly, causing vibration when the wing slots open, as soon as the slots are fully engaged the aircraft will turn steadily without bucking. Many pilots, find this initial vibration disconcerting, claiming it spoils their aim and disorients them, but I believe a veteran pilot will learn to ride out the initial disturbance and cling to his opponent. If the turn is unusually violent and the aircraft stalls, dropping its nose, the slightest forward pressure on the stick will bring it out. Stalls are nearly always predictable and the aircraft will not flip over on its back and begin spinning.

"The 109 dives very well, but although its speed is good, it maneuvers poorly in a prolonged plunge, particularly after high

Fig. 6-1. This Messerschmitt 109G-6/U-2 was presented to the British when its pilot, disoriented, landed on an RAF base by mistake. More Me 109G-6 models were built than any other. Range was 615 miles with drop tank. The G-6/R1 could carry a 550-lb or 1,100-lb bomb in place of the belly tank, and the G-/R2 was fitted with two 21-cm rocket tubes in place of the under-wing cannon for attacks against the massed formations of American bombers.

velocity is reached. In the pull out, however, it has a decided advantage. The 109 can be climbed at very low airspeeds under a sharp angle of attack. In this attitude it rolls and turns very well in either direction and this situation . . . i.e. . . . a steep climb at low speed should be avoided by British fighters opposing it. Furthermore, due to its exceptional acceleration, the 109 will rapidly outrace its opponents in a climb by the application of full throttle. Therefore, if this aircraft should get on your tail in a climbing situation, reverse position, at once, and dive."

Marginally faster than the Spitfire and much faster than the Hurricane, the 109 could also push over and down without its engine cutting out. Lacking direct fuel injection, the engines of the Allied fighters would cough and sputter for a few seconds, when negative forces cut off the flow of fuel.

The 109 was most dangerous to its pilot when diving on its back at high speeds, close to the ground. A quick half roll and dive was a favorite method of eluding pursuit in a dogfight, but in the 109, the elevators became very heavy making a quick pull out virtually impossible. However, at high altitude, the 109 could roll and go down much more quickly that its early Allied counterparts.

With the introduction of the G model (Fig. 6-2), the Messerschmitt suffered by comparison with improved Allied models. Although the G was faster, it was not as maneuverable as the earlier E and F. Its cockpit was filled by with fumes from the engine at low revs. The bulges on either side of the cockpit, which housed the machine gun breeches, restricted airborne vision, and with wing cannon it could hardly maneuver at all. The Spitfire IX now climbed better at all altitudes, and was faster at most. The 109E still dove faster, but the Spitfire not only turned faster but rolled faster. The Spitfire XIV was faster in all categories and the P-51C was also superior, but by a wider margin.

Landing A Challenge

Landing the 109 was always a challenge. The aircraft had a tendency to nose down in the 90 mph approach glide. Any slower than that and the pilot got a queasy sinking feeling, any faster and the aircraft seemed to dive at the runway. During the approach, however, the 109 would turn beautifully at 90 mph. without stalling and with very little loss in altitude. It did not float on final and had to be tucked back into the three point attitude forcibly. The temptation was great to land on the main wheels, but if this were tried, the left wing would drop, the ailerons would be a broken undercarriage or groundloop, at best, a complete disaster at worst.

On the other hand, holding the aircraft off in the three point altitude would assure a successful landing. As in take off, allowing the aircraft to fly itself back to the ground was the best way of avoiding accidents.

During the war in Russia most 109 squadrons operated from grass fields (Fig. 6-3). There, the resilency of the soil forced the

Fig. 6-2. The first of the G series 109s, the Me 109G-1, featured a pressurized cockpit. Power was up to 1,475 hp, giving a maximum speed of 403 mph at 21,300 ft. Empty weight was 5,610 lbs, up to 1,180 lbs over the 1,100-hp E model.

pilots to hit the powerful brakes more quickly in order to control their roll out. However, late in the war, when Major Wilhelm Batz (237 victories) was commanding II/JG 52 in Austria, he lost 39 out of 42 fighters when his group took over a new airbase with concrete runways. As the group came in for their landings, the pilots, not used to the firm foundation of the permanent strip, applied their brakes too quickly and as Batz later recalled, "caused us to lose more aircraft in five minutes than we had lost to the Russians in five months."

—Franz Stigler

I started my flying training with the Messerschmitt Bf 109 at the Luftwaffe Fighter School in the summer of 1942 on both B and D models which were powered with the old Junkers Jumo 210 engine of 600 hp. Later I flew the E variants with the Mercedes DB 600 and 601 before transitioning into the F-2 and F-4 models. In January 1943 I was posted to frontline combat in Russia and was introduced to the Me 109 G-2 model. In May of the same year I changed over to a G-4 and in August to the G-6 variant. From February 1945 until the end of hostitlities I flew G-10s, G-14s, and, finally, the K-4 models of the Me 109. Total flying time on all versions of this aircraft was approximately 1200 hours including 423 frontline combat missions. Of my score of 137 aerial victories with the Me 109, over 100 of them were achieved behind the stick of the G-6 model.

Not Easy To Fly

The Me 109 was not an easy aircraft to fly. In training units many younger pilots had a fear of flying it, due to problems they encountered in their first few missions. These difficulties usually were the result of one of the following:

1. Before 1944 the Luftwaffe did not have a two seat version of the Me 109, nor any other training aircraft with similar flying characteristics. The transition from slow, easy-to-fly planes like the Arado 96 to a fast, unforgiving single seat Me 109 was a memorable experience.

2. Due to the extremely narrow track of the landing gear in combination with the powerful engine and small rudder, the Me 109 had a tendency to swing off the runway during takeoff as soon as the tail wheel lost contact with the ground.

3. The visibility from the cockpit, especially on the ground in a three point attitude, was very restricted.

Fig. 6-3. In Russian, JG 54 (Green Hearts) was part of the Luftwaffe 1st Air Corps, flying Me 109Fs.

4. During training, the Me 109 B, C, D and E models would occasionally make a half roll just before touch down, if . . . when the gear and flaps were down and the aircraft was near stalling its speed . . . the pilot applied full power abruptly. This was extremely unnerving to young pilots, many of whom had gotten into this habit, without paying the penalty, while flying more docile trainers.

The accident rate in training units with the Me 109 was, therefore, terribly high. Relatively long periods of flying were needed to get acquainted with this aircraft; although, after this phase was passed, the experienced pilot discovered that the aircraft was really not at all tricky or dangerous—once he understood its characteristics.

The Me 109 was also said to be less maneuverable than comparable Allied fighters such as the Hurricane, Spitfire, Yak, or Mustang. I do not believe this to be quite true.

The F series and later models had rounded wing tips which improved the aircraft's basic turning capability. Inexperienced pilots were often afraid to attempt a steep, narrow turn, as the plane shook violently, a result of the automatic wing slots engaging. In addition the pressure on the stick was very high. However, I found that due to the slots, the aircraft's stalling characteristics were better than those of other comparable Allied planes I flew and although it may be argued, I found that I was able to outmaneuver Laggs, Yaks and even Spitfires in dogfights.

The performance of the Me 109 was up-to-date until the end of 1942 or beginning of 1943. In the war's final years the aircraft's capability fell more and more in comparison to the new Allied planes. I think the Me 109 reached its final stage of development with F-4 model as the succeeding models offered little or no improvement. The construction was solid and sturdy enough—I survived several dives in excess of 570 mph. The airframe was relatively resistant to enemy gunfire, but this was not true of the engine and cooling system. In July of 1944, for instance, my G-6 was caught in a dogfight with Yaks and took three 30mm hits, one each in the right wing, rear fuselage and in the horizontal stabilizer, yet I was able to fly back to base with ease, the aircraft showing no sign of breaking up.

The DB 605A 12-cylinder V-engine was, in my opinion, a sound design, its main advantage against its competition being its fuel injection capability. The main reason for the troubles and failures we later experienced might have been due to the quality of the materials available to us as the war progressed. In this connection, I can remember very well the Americans flying their Mustangs over the Atlantic to Europe. At the time, I could not believe it. The endurance of all our Me 109 Models was far too short, even with 300 liter (78 gallon) auxiliary tanks below the fuselage.

Weak Armament

The greatest disadvantage of the Me 109 was its weak armament. The best combination existed on the E model which was equipped with a pair of slow firing, Oerlikon-built, Becker-designed 20mm MG-FF in the wings and two synchronized Rheinmetall 7.9mm MG 17 machine guns in the nose cowling. For its day, the E model was a superior warplane, and in this respect the F and G models were a step backwards. They originally had only a single 15mm MG 151/15 cannon firing through the propeller shaft and two light 7.9mm MG 17 machine guns in the cowling as in the Me 109E. From the G-4 model on, the 7.9mm guns were replaced by 13mm MG 131 machine guns, the large breeches of which caused those telltale bulges on the late variant Me 109s , while the cannon was up gunned to 20mm. This armament was sufficient for dogfighting, but, with only one cannon, not nearly adequate in attacks on bomber formations. There also were special versions of the G model which carried two additional MG 151/20 cannons on pylons below the wings. We called them *Kanonen-boot*. These extra cannon worked out well in bomber attacks, but the aircraft's maneuverability and performance suffered so considerably with this addition, that no Luftwaffe pilot was very interested in flying it, not with escorting fighters around.

Although the Rheinmetall MG 131 fired a 13mm bullet, roughly equivalent to an American .50 caliber round, the 109 F and G, with only a pair of these and one 20mm cannon, in many of their production configurations, suffered from lack of firepower when compared to the six and, sometimes, eight gun batteries to be found on the American P-51 and /47 fighters.

The MG 131 had several advantages, however. It weighed only 40 lbs., had a high rate of fire, approaching 1000 rounds per minute, and it pumped its shots out at a high velocity of 2,560 feet per second. Nevertheless, the Mauser MG 151/120 cannon was a superior weapon.

Originally designed as 15mm heavy machine gun in competition with the 13mm Rheinmetall weapon, it proved so promising that it was rechambered to fire 20mm cannon shells. In its final configuration it weighed only 93 lbs. and its rate of fire was better than those of most machine guns (750 rounds per minute) and it had a velocity 30 feet per second better than the MG 131.

To give one an idea of how much fire-power this cannon possessed, in one minute it could theoretically discharge nearly 200 lbs. of metal at the enemy, although no German aircraft cannon ever carried more than 200 rounds per gun, roughly enough for 5 seconds of non-stop firing.

The G-10 and K-4 models had a Rheinmetall 30mm MK 108 cannon instead of the 20mm gun. The efficiency of this weapon was enormous. A single hit on a two-engine aircraft meant almost sure destruction. However the trajectory of the gun was much too curved due to its short barrel and low, 1600 ft. per second velocity, thus the accuracy was not very good. The rate of technical failures was also very high, due to the weapon's cheap, stamping manufacture. I personally preferred the old 20mm gun.

A very dubious modification to the Me 109 was the addition of the so-called "Galland Hood" in 1944. The visibility was much better with the new deisgn, but the emergency release of the one piece canopy had a high rate of failure. Based on my personal experience and in discussions with other pilots, I estimate the failure of the release to run as high as 50 percent. I was twice forced to ride my Me 109 down to a quick crash landing, hoping all the way to be able to jar the hood loose before the plane exploded. Both times I was lucky enough to escape the burning aircraft as the shock of the crash freed the canopy mechanism. This type of corrective action is, however, not looked upon with great favor by a figher pilot.

In spite of all my complaints and the plane's many deficiencies, I liked the Me 109 very much. I never felt quite at home in any other aircraft as I did in the old *Beule*—which translates as *tin-boil*.

The best fighters I faced were the P-51 Mustang and the Russian Yak-9U. Both types had a clear advantage in performance over the Me 109, regardless of variant, and this includes the K-4 with its 2000 hp. engine. The Mustang was unsurpassed in speed and in its high altitude performance, while the Yak-9U was the champion in climbing ability and maneuverability. The Curtiss P-40 was a relatively easy adversary. The plane was fast enough, but in climbing and maneuvering it was very marginal. I am sure that my judgment is not entirely objective, however, as I had to face only Russian flown P-40s and it is quite possible that the pilots were not very accustomed to this aircraft. (Other German aces, flying against the British over North Africa, found the P-40 very quick in turns.)

Pilot Training

This brings up a very important point I must make clear. More important than the quality of the aircraft was the quality of the pilot. In the last months of the war I feel the American pilot had the highest level of training and his ability showed it. However, the finest pilots I ever faced were the members of the Units of Guards of the Russian Air Force. In 1943 they flew Yaks as well as Bell P-39 Aircobras and later flew the Yak-9U only. Most of them painted their entire cowl red, much in the same manner as Luftwaffe aircraft during the Battle of Britain. These pilots were a concentration of the most highly skilled and courageous fighters in the Soviet Air Force and during the war, we were told it took a minimum of 10 victories to gain eligibility to such units.

Another Luftwaffe pilot and ace, Franz Stigler who flew with Hans Marseilles and JG 27 in North Africa, as well as Adolf Galland's all ace squadron, JV-44, at war's end, also chooses the Messerchmitt 109F as his favorite.

Franz scored 28 confirmed victories against the RAF and the USAF in 480 combat missions. Among his victims were practically every type of fighter and daylight bomber used by the Western Allies. Balancing out his 28 victories in everything from the 109 to the Me 262 jet fighter, Franz Stigler was shot down an incredible 17 times, bailing out six times and crash landing or ditching on the remaining occasions.

He started out with JG 27 in Libya and fought throughout the

North African campaign into Tunisia, Italy, and then saw combat over Germany in defense of the Reich until war's end.

My philosophy as a fighter pilot was a simple one. Hit first, hit hard, and get out as quickly as you can. Better five seconds yellow than a long time dead.

I preferred the 109F because it flew well at any altitude, was as fast as most, actually faster than the G, had a superior rate of climb and could dive very well. Most of all, it instilled confidence in its pilot. Like others in my group, I flew the 109 without wing guns, whenever possible. This made it considerably lighter and far more maneuverable. The 20mm MG 151 cannon firing through the spinner and the two cowl mounted machine guns in the F and G were very effective against other fighters and all we pilots felt was really needed. Later on, when the G model also incorporated two additional cannon in the wing, the aircraft became very sluggish and most pilots felt that the added firepower was more than offset by the loss of maneuverability.

In Africa the performance of aircraft on both sides was badly affected by the need to tropicalize the engines to cope with blowing sand and grit. Comparing their performance with those on the Western Front, is like matching a tug against a motor torpedo boat. Even so, the problem was the same for both sides . . . either tropicalize or not fly.

My first combat was against British flown Curtiss P40s. It was then I discovered how quickly they could turn. We started our attack from the classic position and were coming down on their rear from above. Before I knew what was happening, they had turned back into us with all of their six wing guns smoking. I panicked, jerked back on the stick and climbed like a madman, my fist in the engine for more power. I must have gone up at least 5,000 ft. before I leveled off and began looking around. I was lost. Luckily my *rotte* leader found me and we went home.

Like the Hurricane, the P-40 was hard to shoot down. The Hurricane simply absorbed bullets that passed through its fabric, but the P-40 was as tough as boiler plate. Unless you struck the engine or the pilot, it kept on going and it could turn like a racing pony. We soon learned never, never dog fight with them if at all possible. Our 109Fs were much faster, however, and we could climb far better. We could also dive much more quickly, but the P-40 like the P-47 which came after it, eventually would catch you in a dive, if it was long enough.

We were usually outnumbered in the desert and as with most

fighter pilots, our tactics were to surprise the enemy by diving out of the sun, if possible, fire and pull away, then climb back for another attack. This all sounds simple and elementary, but it is good advice. Simple concepts usually are.

There were very few Spitfires in the desert, at first, and we feared their reputation from the Battle of Britain. After we shot some down, this anxiety evaporated. Our first victims were Mark Vs and they were no match for the 109F, except in a dogfight, so we simply avoided that type of combat. When the Allies landed in North Africa, Sicily and Italy, we met the Spitfire IX and they were completely different. We had a very bad time with them since their speed had jumped nearly 50 mph., and they were now carrying 20mm cannon.

Fortunately for us the R.A.F., in particular, used to fly very unwieldy formations and we almost always spotted them first. They used a constant turning and weaving which caused the sun to glint off their aircraft, and in the desert this unintentional signalling could be spotted for 20 miles, giving us the chance to climb above them and attack out of the sun. The British also were prone to employing weavers, who flew above their line abreast and line astern formations of four to six aircraft. These pilots must have been inexperienced, because they were relatively easy to shoot down. We always went for them first, and often wondered why the R.A.F. placed their newer pilots in such jeopardy, entrusting them with clearing their formations. In the Luftwaffe, the opposite would have been the case, with experienced pilots used to clear and scout.

The Hurricane was also a difficult fighter to shoot down. We never knew the difference between the Mark Is and IIs. As far as we were concerned they were just Hurricanes. The difference in performance we attributed to the ability of the pilots flying them. In addition to our bullets going right on through it, the Hurricane was extremely maneuverable. Our 109s were faster, but the Hurricane was much easier to fly and had no bad habits. It was also very heavily armed with four 20mm cannon. However, although it could turn inside of us, we soon discovered that it could not fire its cannon in a steep bank. The recoil from the first burst would stall the aircraft, causing it to snap over the top.

In North Africa we also encountered the Bell P-39 Airacobra. Our pilots had no trouble with it at all. They were always below us and it was simply a case of diving on them, firing and pulling up for another attack.

The P-38 Lightning amazed us. Our intelligence had no information about them and when first met, we were cautious and a little worried because we did not know what to expect. Their pilots also flew clumsy formations.

At first, these were pretty much straight and level. We almost always surprised them and then quickly broke away. Our first pass would break them up pretty well and we would then go after the singles. It was then we learned how dangerous they were. They could turn inside us with ease and they could go from level flight to climb almost instantaneously. We lost quite a few pilots who tried to make an attack and then pull up. The P-38s were on them at once. They closed so quickly that there was little one could do except to roll quickly and dive down, for while the P-38 could turn inside us, it rolled very slowly through the first five or ten degrees of bank, and by then we would already be gone.

One cardinal rule we never forgot was: Avoid fighting a P-38 head on. That was suicide. Their armament was so heavy and their firepower so murderous, that no one ever tried that type of attack more than once.

After the first few encounters with them, the pilots of the P-38s began flying an overlapping weaving formation which again, because of reflecting sun rays, soon gave them away. However, these twin engined machines were so big that we would sit above them and marvel at how they could manage to turn and twist so much without colliding. One reason we continued to surprise them must have been the fact that they were so busy weaving in and out, that they had no time to watch for the enemy.

This new tactic did provide them with more mobility, however, and they could break into our attacks a little better, so we now came down on them from two directions simultaneously.

When I was transferred to a squadron for home defense against heavy four engined bombers with their fighter escorts, I finally met the P-47 and, later, the P-51. My recollections of these two aircraft are not happy ones. There were so many of them, it was hard to get at the bombers and during the last year of the war, American fighters were all around us. The P-47 wasn't so bad because we could out turn and out climb it, initially. But that big American fighter could roll with deceiving speed and when it came down on you in a long dive, there was no way you could get away from it. It must have had a huge brick built into it, somewhere.

Look Alike

In addition to inflicting tremendous punishment, it could absorb an incredible amount of our firepower and still fly. The P-51 was something else. It was an awful antagonist, in the truest sense of that word and we hated it. It could do everything we could do and do it much better. First off, it was hard to recognize. Unless you saw it from the side, it looked like a 109. This caused us trouble from the outset. We would see them, think they were ours and then have the damned things shoot us full of holes. We didn't like them at all!

The bombers they protected were relatively easy to shoot down, once you discovered how to attack them and how to evade their escorts. I learned the hard way that you do not attack a B-17 from the rear. I was shot down three times by B-17 tail gunners and still have a scar on my leg and a hole in my forehead from .50 caliber bullets fired by them. It took me that long to learn to come down from above and go through the formation, straight down and from the side, diving into the clear, before climbing back and again up to one side for another overhead attack. The only other acceptable method was from directly head on. But these were usually attempted by special, heavily armed Fw 190s equipped with 30mm cannon and additional armor plating over their engines and wing leading edges. Furthermore, these tactics were based on mass asaults of from ten to fifty aircraft, in line abreast, all attempting to knock out the formation leaders. As such, heavy armor and armament was called for, maneuverability was secondary.

When the 109 was laden with extra firepower, usually in the form of wing emplaced, gondola type cannon fairings, it suffered drastically from reduced maneuverability and was transformed into a relatively easy mark for escorting fighters.

During the war I had the opportunity to fly captured P-47s and P-51s. I didn't like the Thunderbolt. It was too big. The cockpit was immense and unfamiliar. After so many hours in the snug confines of the 109, everything felt out of reach and too far away from the pilot. Although the P-51 was a fine ariplane to fly, because of its reactions and capabilities, it too was disconcerting. With all those levers, controls and switches in the cockpit, I'm surprised your pilots could find the time to fight. We had nothing like this in the 109. Everything was simple and very close to the pilot. You fitted into the cockpit like a hand in a glove. Our instrumentation was complete, but simple: throttle, mixture control and prop pitch.

How your pilots were able to work all their gadgets and still function, amazes me.

The 109 was my airplane and although it eventually received a more sinister reputation, I didn't care too much for the Fw 190. It was very good and very fast at low level in its initial type, but poor at altitude. This was somewhat corrected in later models, but never fully remedied. It was faster than the 109, but we had a better cruise. It was also more modern and had far better ground handling capabilities, was heavier and possessed of a more powerful engine. However, a majority of veteran pilots preferred to fly the 109 and remained with it, even when large stocks of the Fw 190 became available. The Fw 190 had more firepower, but two of its guns (20mm cannon) were located in the wings, outboard. High G forces often caused them to malfunction and jam. In the 109, your guns were connected on a central axis. If your aim was off a bit, you missed, but if you were careful, this central battery had tremendous impact.

In my opinion, newer, less experienced pilots probably preferred the Fw 190 for this very reason. Firing from a relatively stable position, its armament performed satisfactorily. But stable positions are not often encountered in aerial combat. It is the ability to attack from the odd, disoriented position that often spells the difference between victory and defeat in a dogfight. Veterans with a great deal of combat time soon appreciated this fact, which only became evident with experience. It is for this reason that many preferred the 109's gun arrangement and did not like that aircraft when wing guns were added. It also caused them to choose the 109 over the Fw 190. Flying the 109 was more demanding, but a proficient marksman could do more with that airplane.

—Walter Wolfrum

Colonel Herbert Kaiser who recently retired from the West German Air Force, was only one of 24 to pass the strenuous and exhaustive physical and written tests for acceptance to primary sea-flight instruction in 1936. At Puetnitz he was introduced to the Focke-Wulf Stoesser, the Heinkel He 51, and the Arado 68. Although the planes were slow, they were forgiving, and allowed the inexperienced pilot to profit by his mistakes, providing an excellent platform to indulge in stunt flying. Kaiser graduated with a certificate qualifying him for both land and sea based aircraft and was transferred to the Fighter School at Werneuchen, near Berlin, for advanced training and assignment. It was here that he was introduced to the plane he was to pilot for the next seven years, the Messerschmitt Me 109. It was not as cordial as the docile trainers, but he was to score 68 confirmed aerial victories with it.

As Colonel Kaiser describes it: "The Me 109B was not an easy aircraft to fly. It had to be directed with utmost attention from the split-second one gave it gas. The extremely narrow tracked under-carriage could not fully compensate for the normal tendency of the aircraft to pull to the right due to the prop torque. The maintaining of one's starting direction could be accomplished only by the smooth application of power, the balancing of the rudder, and the balancing of the elevators to lift the tail only after airborne in order to keep constant aileron efficiency. Any casual disregard for these basic rules had a result of breaking the flight path and possible crash."

"The cardinal rule during landing was that at the point of touchdown the gear and tail skid had to be oriented in the line of projected roll without further attempt at directional control. Separation of the aerodynamic lift due to insufficient approach speed, and excessive directional corrections performed during the landing procedure was the most common cause of crashes. The experienced pilot had these rules in his flesh and blood and this enabled him to make better use of his time by concentrating on other matters."

"Visibility from the cockpit was good, although during takeoff it was quite restricted in the frontal area until the tail wheel left the ground. It was not at all reassuring to look forward and see only the large metal cowl, and this was why the aircraft had to be correctly oriented on take off.

"Although the Me 109B was useful as a frontline combat aircraft and far out-classed enemy aircraft of the time in speed and climbing ability, its initial Junkers-built engine was extremely sensitive and not sufficiently powered."

"The Luftwaffe did not, in my estimation, have a truly superior and robust fighter aircraft until the appearance of the Me 109E. The use of the DB 601 engine with 1200 hp, the increased speed, and the high climb rate made the Me 109E, in relation to her counterparts, the best fighter of her time. Her armament of two machine guns and three cannon were more than enough to knock any enemy plane out of the air with a well placed burst of fire."

Under the leadership and instruction of Captain Hannes Trautloft (later General and Kommodore of JC 54 "Green Hearts"), Kaiser completed his training and on July 1, 1938 was posted to

2/132 (2n *staffel* of Fighter Wing 132) in Jever under the command of Major Carl Schumacher. His *staffel* leader at this time was one Johannes Steinhoff who was to become one of the Luftwaffe's greatest leaders and who today is a General in the New German Air Force at NATO Headquarters in Brussels, Belgium.

In the fall of 1938, Kaiser's unit was assigned to support the occupation of the Sudentenland flying Me 109s. A struggle with the Czechs was expected, but much to his dismay, Kaiser found no aircraft rising to his challenge. Shortly after the occupation, Kaiser was posted to a carrier group in Keil-Holtenau, a large harbor on the Baltic Sea. This group was to be composed of a Me 109B fighter *staffel*, and a Ju 87 Stuka dive bombing staffel, however, the initial training was carried out with specially equipped Heinkel He 50s. These slow speed training planes had arrestor hooks added to them in order to familiarize the pilots with the tactics of carrier landings and take-offs before they tried it with the faster, more tempermental, Me 109s. Take-offs and landings were conducted on a giant outlined landing surface in Travemuende which was rigged with arresting wires and recovery gear to simulate the deck of the German Navy's aircraft carrier *Graf Zeppelin*, then under construction.

When the decision was made by the German ministry not to build the *Graf Zeppelin*, Kaiser and his fighter *staffel* were transferred to East Prussia for the upcoming invasion of Poland. On September 1, 1939 at 6:00 p.m. they took to the air for their first real combat mission. Their orders were to provide cover escort for the advanced Stuka flights whose target was the Polish Navy's anchorage at Hela in the Bay of Danzig. Although flak was heavy from the Polish anti-aircraft batteries surrounding the harbor, no aerial opposition was encountered due mostly to the surprise of the attack.

On September 20, 1939 Kaiser's unit was pulled back and transferred to Cuxhaven, in Germany. From here he flew continuous patrol duty and cover flights over the Heligoland Bight (German Bay) now mounted in the Me 109E. On May 6th Kaiser achieved his first victory while carrying out an interception mission with his wingman. Vectored to intercept two Royal Air Force Bristol Blenheims approaching the coast, the *rotte* sighted the Blenheims, but were in turn spotted by the RAF bombers who quickly turned toward home, wanting no part of an engagement with the approaching 109s. Giving chase, Kaiser and his wingman caught the Blenheims near the Isle of Terschelling and destroyed them. The next day he was decorated with the German Iron Cross 2nd Class.

On May 10, 1940 Kaiser, now flying as part of III/JG 77 took part in the start of the Western Campaign against airfields in Holland and was credited with the destruction of two Dutch Fokker D 21s. He was then sent to France where he remained, flying patrol until the Dunkirk encirclement.

Of these days Kaiser relates: "Although prior to the start of the Western Campaign in May 1940, no German pilot could make a comprehensive comparison between British and French fighters and our ME 109E, we firmly believed we had the best airplane based on comparative flying reports and an abundance of rumors. Personally, at the advent of hostilities, I had contact only with Dutch Fokker D 21s, and, this fixed geared monoplane, approximately 50 mph slower than a 109E, offered no particular challenge. Some of my comrades from neighboring units, however, had encountered the RAF Spitfires and Hurricanes, as well as the French Dewoitines and Morane Saulniers and affirmed what we all had believed about our aircraft."

"In personally facing the RAF in the air over the Dunkirk encirclement, I found that the Me 109E was faster, possessed a higher rate of climb, but was somewhat less maneuverable than the RAF fighters. Nevertheless, during the campaign, no Spitfire or Hurricane ever turned inside of my plane, and after the war the RAF admitted the loss of 450 Hurricanes during the Battle of France.

From Dunkirk Kaiser and III/JG 77 were posted to Norway where they stayed until August 30th without any combat encounters. It was then back to Berlin-Doeberitz inside Germany to await assignment. For the next two months he was relieved of duty and reported for the filming of *Kampfgeschwader Leutzow* (The Leutzow Fighter Wing), a propaganda film to be shown to both the Luftwaffe recruits as well as the German public. In this epic, Kaiser received his first chance to fly an enemy aircraft when he piloted a Curtiss P-36 in which he played the part of an allied attacker. He, of course, lost this aerial battle to one of the Luftwaffe's own.

In late 1940, Kaiser, who had returned to III/JF 77, was transferred to Northern France (flying defensive sorties from Britanny against increasing R.A.F. bombing raids. In March 1941, the unit was again reassigned, this time to Rumania as part of a protective umbrella around the critical oil fields, and on April 6th flew the first combat mission against the Yugoslav Air Force. Here Kaiser engaged in some interesting encounters, as the Yugoslavs were also piloting the Me 109E, but with much less training or experience. This fact, in addition to numerical superiority quickly swung the advantage in the Luftwaffe's favor.

From Rumania, III/JG 77 next went to Greece where for the two weeks prior to the campaign against the Isle of Crete (May 20, 1941) Kaiser flew continuous combat patrol and interdiction raids against the earthen fortifications of the island. On one of these missions he encountered and shot down an R.A.F. Westland Lysander, but the British and Greek air defenses were woefully understrengthened and his unit met little aerial opposition.

On the day of the invasion, Kaiser flew escort duty of the Junkers Ju 52 paratroop drops at Crete/Malemis keeping enemy artillery and ground forces busy. On the 22nd the unit was moved to a base at Crete/Malemis and continued to fly strafing and ground attack missions against the remaining British forces. On May 30th the unit was returned to Rumania to refit and repair outside Bucharest. Then came Operation Barbarossa—the invasion of Russia.

Eastern Front

One June 19, 1941 III/JG 77 was posted to Bacau on the Russian border and on the 21st engaged in their first missions against the Russian Air Force. Taking off at 4:00 a.m. Kaiser achieved his initial kill over the Eastern Front later in the day near Balti.

Colonel Kaiser recalls the Russian compaign: "Against the early Russian aircraft the Me 109E was untouchable. The Soviet planes were slower and could not climb with us. They were, however, highly maneuverable, especially the I-15 and I-16, and one could not allow an encounter to deteriorate into a contest of turns. This was easily avoided, because we always had the element of surprise, due to our high speed and advanced communication systems."

"In Russia I encountered many varied aircraft, particularly bombers, for the most part the twin engined Ilyusin DB-3, and later the Pe-2, and IL-2 attack bombers. The greatest losses for the Soviets, at least in our sector, occurred with the DB-3. A military version of a Soviet long distance record-breaker, it had great range, but was incredibly slow, and possessed poor defensive firepower. All weapons were hand-held, rifle-caliber guns and the bomber was blind to a direct tail on approach. A single burst between the left engine and the fuselage into the wing root and the unprotected fuel tanks, guaranteed immediate burning and unavoidable crash. It was considerably more difficult to attack the Pe-2 because of her speed, twin-tail assembly and the unrestricted tail gunner's vision."

The Ilyushin IL-2—Stormovik—was also tough. A single engine fighter bomber, not exceptionally fast, but very well armored, this plane required a detailed knowledge of its construction and a well executed approach to destroy. The unforgettable Moelders showed me personally how one downed this aircraft. The IL-2 possessed head armour behind the pilot; but just behind this armour was a small tank which was utilized as a starter cartridge. Totally unprotected and vulnerable, this tank was exploded with a single incendiary burst. Of course, in this mode of attack, a precise and accurate burst was necessary. Later the Soviets installed a rear gunner's position and armored the starter cartridge."

"During my participation in the Russian campaign, I also encountered the Lagg 3 and the Mig 3. I did destroy some of these, but it would be extremely difficult to make any well founded comparison with the Me 109 because of my limited confrontation."

Following the thrust of the German Army, Kaiser and III/JG 77 arrived in the Crimea where they continued their duel with the Soviet air forces. They were now flying Me 109 Fs. During the crossing of the Dnieper River, upon returning from a recon flight over the area, Kaiser sighted a group of 27 Martin Maryland bombers (lend-lease aircraft) and destroyed three of them, attacking the formation from below and behind.

From the Crimea, Kaiser flew over Sebastopol in December 1941 and over Kursk in January 1942, his first winter campaign. Despite the freezing Russian winter, by June he had raised his victory total to 46, at which time he was transferred north for the second push on Moscow. The second summer of war in Russia resulted in stalemate and with the arrival of an early winter, Kaiser and III/JG 77 were again transferred, this time to Africa, arriving at Tobruk on October 20th.

North Africa

It was in North Africa that Kaiser received his first Me 109G; "Here I was introduced to the Me 109G which had an even more powerful engine than the F model and a larger compressor (supercharger). It also had extremely good high altitude performance. The air density of the North African sky was considerably less than that over Russia, and our performance could be maintained only through the constant use of the compressor. From a pure flying standpoint, the Me 109G offered little over the Me 109F. She was considerably heavier and still had the difficult take off and landing qualities inherent with all the Me 109 variants."

"During the African campaign, we were short of aircraft and for the young pilots with little actual air or combat experience, it was very difficult to master the 109. In addition, landings and takeoffs were aggravated by the general condition of the desert air strips, not to mention sand and blowing grit. Because of these conditions, the relatively few number of flight worthy planes were usually flown by the older, more experienced pilots, and the appearance of the same familiar names dominated the victory totals."

From Tobruk, the unit moved back to El Alamein, but Kaiser requested to stay behind for an extra day in order to visit an old friend before leaving. When Kaiser finally took off in company with his wingman, who also had remained he encountered a group of six Curtiss P-40s strafing the Tobruk supply routes. He recalls this action very vividly; "I had flown about a half a mile when I sighted the enemy formation of P-40s strafing a convoy on the main German supply route into Tobruk. I would not have even noticed the RAF formation if it had not been for the geysers of dirt and sand their shells were kicking up around the convoy. At first glance I still could not make out how many of the enemy there were, due to the blending of the camouflage with the desert setting below. Finally I was able to identify the P-40s making single file strafing runs and turned to the attack. They were so intent on their work they failed to notice me. I drove on the last aircraft from above and behind letting him have a short burst. As my shells ripped into his aircraft and he went down, the pilot must have managed to radio the rest of the flight, for they immediately made a steep left turn and headed out into the desert in a zig-zagging pattern, their formation appearing like a snake on the desert floor. Within about 40 miles, I caught up with them and again pressed home an attack which resulted in the destruction of a second P-40. In the heat of the battle, however, I became reckless and as I watched the second P-40 crash into the sand I noticed flashes across my wing. Another of the RAF aircraft had gotten on my tail and was pouring fire into my fuselage and wings, disabling my oil and water systems, I pulled my Me 109G into a steep turn and looked for a place to put my aircraft down as I was too low to bail out. As my plane skidded across the sand, the dust was so thick I couldn't tell if I was on fire or not. Fortunately, for me, the aircraft did not burn."

Reported Dead

Kaiser's wingman, who was also engaged in aerial combat, mistook the flying dust for smoke and upon landing at the unit's new base in El Alamein, reported the death of his commander. Kaiser, however, after a four hour hike across the sand, reached the main Tobruk supply road, where he was picked up by German forces and returned to his base at El Alamein much to the surprise of his comrades.

Between October 28th and November 5th, he accounted for four more enemy planes, but was himself wounded and sent to Athens for two weeks to recover. He rejoined the group on November 21, 1942 in Berigahzi and on his return to flying status quickly shot down a Spitfire V.

Describing the tactics employed by the Luftwaffe in North Africa in late 1942 and his impressions of some of the aircraft he faced, Colonel Kaiser relates; "The classic dogfight was still partly used in Africa, and the lone sortie was prevalent. We were forced to this lone sortie tactic of surprise due to the overwhelming supply of Allied aircraft and, in this way, were able to spread ourselves over more area. Any other tactics would be coupled with high losses on our side, a condition we could not allow. Additionally, the speed and durability of the Me 109G lent itself very well to this type of tactic. If we were overmatched, we could always break off."

"The Curtiss P-40 was not as fast as the Me 109G and in a confrontation with this plane we had nothing to worry about as long as the basic rules of combat tactics were followed. We did, however, have to avoid getting into the middle of a large formation, for the P-40 turned well and, as an old German saying goes "Too many dogs are the death of the rabbit."

"The P-38 Lightning was equal to our Me 109G in performance, far superior in range, and was a much more difficult adversary in a dogfight. However, I never employed any special evasive maneuvers when I encountered one of them. Evasive tactics, as far as I am concerned, were dictated by the situation and were a reflex reaction. For the most part, independent of the aircraft on your tail, one would utilize a steep turn and pull out to get behind his enemy, or pull up on the stick in a succession of stuttering steps to reduce speed, hoping the abrupt velocity decrease would not be picked up in time by the aircraft behind you, forcing him to fly by exposing his belly. I always considered a turn out and dive a high risk tactic and, to my knowledge, this particular move was not used to any great extent by Luftwaffe figher pilots."

In January 1943, Kaiser was detached from JG 77 and sent to a replacement depot in Southern France as an instructor. He stayed here for four months before rejoining III/JG 77 on the Island of Sardinia. He was then transferred within the wing to I/JG 77 and posted to Italy where he destroyed four more aircraft. Then in January 1944, Kaiser was returned to Germany for a routine medical checkup after which he was assigned to I/JG 1 under the command of Colonel Walter Oesau. With this unit he flew until June 6, 1944 in the Defense of the Reich. From June 6th until August 9th he was stationed on the Normandy Front flying in a defensive role against the allied invasion forces and describes his experiences as follows:

"Near the end of June 1944 while attached to I/JG 1, on an airfield just outside Paris, France, an excellent example of the almost complete Allied air superiority occured. I was vectored out to intercept an incoming flight of Allied bombers which was attacking our troops in the Normandy area. Our take-off had to be only in the smallest of flights (usually 2 to 4 aircraft) due to the Allied fighters which almost always waited above the bases for our fighters to emerge from cloud cover. We would be forced to sneak from our base into our target area by hedge hopping over the terrain to take advantage of all the camouflage possible. Flying only a few feet off the ground kept us off radar screens, but sometimes put us on the side of a hill. We would only climb to heights when we reached the attack point under the enemy planes."

"My flight of four aircraft sighted a formation of escorting Spitfires, and we positioned ourselves to engage them. We were instead caught by a second group of Allied fighters and in the process I lost my three men. Escape from the onslaught seemed impossible. Only because of my experience and the lucky appearance of a nearby cloud was I able to save myself."

"At this time the Luftwaffe was being ground into the earth. One could not count on his hand the days he expected to live. It was surprising to me that the Luftwaffe pilot had any nerve left at all, let alone the ability to prepare himself for combat with the enemy under these conditions."

On August 9th Kaiser himself was shot down and badly wounded. On this day his *staffel* was vectored to intercept a formation of approximately 300 Allied aircraft. In preparing for the attack on the RAF Lancaster bombers in the Allied flight, he was jumped from the sun and hit by a Spitfire. He hurriedly opened the canopy of his burning Me 109G and bailed out only to entangle his right leg in his parachute shroud. Badly wounded and with a multiple fracture of his right thigh, he landed behind German lines and remained in a hospital inside Germany until February 1945 at which time he joined Adolf Galland's famous JV 44 flying the Me 262 jet from Munich-Reim. Unable to control the new aircraft due to his still sensitive leg injuries, Kaiser remained with the unit and directed the wing's aircraft to enemy formations from the ground control center.

On May 7th the unit surrendered at Salzburg to advancing American forces, but Kaiser and a fellow pilot escaped and made their way back to Munich on foot where he reached a discharge station and was mustered out of the Luftwaffe. On July 30th he reached his home town of Jessen.

Number of Missions Increased

Colonel Kaiser sums up his wartime career by saying: "In all, I flew over 1,400 combat sorties over enemy territory. While in Poland and during the early Western Campaign these missions were limited. However, after 1941 the number of missions per day increased to two and sometimes three a day depending on the particular situation that we faced, and of course on the weather. In late 1944 and into early 1945 every one of our pilots on active combat duty, veteran or not, was flying three to four missions every single day for as long as his body and mind could take these exhaustive conditions. Some flew even more."

"Except for my time in Africa where supply lines were long and the conditions abnormal, I can not complain about the shortage of replacement parts or the technical maintenance our aircraft received. I always had a very high respect and trust for my ground crew and cannot remember ever having a problem with their ability or dedication to both myself and our Me 109. The supply of new planes, however, was not at all times what I would consider comfortable. It usually just kept up with the demand."

Unlike American aircraft machine guns, German machine guns and aircraft cannon went through a series of important and massive changes during the course of World War II. The Germans began by arming their Messerschmitt 109Bs and Cs with small caliber 7.9mm MG machine guns. Equivalent to an American or English weapon of .30 caliber, the MG 17 had its beginning as an infantry weapon (MG13) and was adapted to aircraft use because of its high rate of fire, up to 1,000 rounds per minute. Manufactured by Rheinmetall, the MG 17 went through several variations, including the MG 15 series, and was used as both a fixed and a flexible aircraft gun. The Messerschmitt 109E mounted a pair of them over its cowling.

Although the MG 17s had a high muzzle velocity of over 2,800 ft. per second, their penetrating power left something to be desired and they were replaced on the 109 G-5 midway through that model's production run, by a pair of Rheinmetall MG 131 machine guns. These belt-fed air-cooled weapons were incredibly light, weighing only 40 lbs., and fired a 13mm cartridge, roughly equivalent to .50 caliber, at a high velocity of 2,560 f.p.s.

However, before these were installed a new gun from Mauser made its appearance. Known as the MG 151/15, it had been built to improve on the relatively low velocity 20mm FF cannon built by Oerlikon and known as the 20mm FF aircraft cannon. Designed by Becker, the Oerlikon MK FF (for machine cannon) was first introduced on the 109D, which mounted it to fire through the propeller hub. The later 109E production models also carried one in each wing. These fired 450 rounds per minute at a rate of 1,680 ft. per second.

Although its cartridge was one third smaller at 15mm, the shell from the Mauser-built MG 151 had a velocity of 2,500 ft. per second and could be fired at a rate of 700 rounds per minute. It was installed in the 109F-2, but because of the design's promise, it was re-bored to accommodate 20mm ammunition and the MG 151, became known as the MG 151/20, making its first appearance in the 109F-4. In its completed version the MG 151/20 weighed only 93 lbs. and had a muzzle velocity of 2,600 ft. per second with a rate of fire of 750 rounds per minute, making it one of the finest aircraft guns of the war.

The 109F-1 began operations with a pair of 7.9mm MG 17 machine guns and a slow firing, low velocity MG FF Oerlikon cannon mounted in the nose. In the F-2, the Oerlikon was replaced by a high velocity MG 151 weapon of 15mm. Roughly .60 caliber, it was not classed as a cannon, but had an exceptionally high rate of fire and better trajectory through higher velocity. As has been noted, in the F-4, this gun was replaced by a bonafide 20mm cannon, developed from the original MG 151 15, and known as the MG 151 15/20. In German ordnance, anything smaller than 20mm has the prefix MG for *maschinen gewehr* MG (machine gun). Weapons over 20mm become *maschinen kanon* MK (machine cannon). Since this weapon was developed from the MG 151 15 heavy machine gun, the MG prefix of its original designation was retained.   —*Herbert Kaiser*

Chapter 7

The Messerschmitt 163 Rocket Fighter

Note: By mid-1944 with Germany's industry breaking up under the hammer blows of Allied bombing attacks. it was imperative that fighters for defense be given the number one production priority. Unfortunately, for the few farseeing Luftwaffe planners, this eleventh hour switch came too late, particularly for Germany's new jet and rocket-powered fighters. Short of fuel, trained personnel and fully equipped facilities, the Me 163 Komet never achieved its potential.□

The first combat ready Komet, the Me 163BV14 (VD+EW) arrived at Zwischenahn in January. Rudy Opitz test flew it in preparation for the first simulated operational mission. A bomber formation was projected as approaching between 20,000 and 26,000 feet. "Pitz" took off in the V14 and made a simulated approach from the rear but upon reaching 20,000 feet the Komet flamed out as it was eased into level flight. If this had happened in a combat situation, the 163 would have been an easy target for Allied fighters, since two minutes were required to restart the Walter engine.

With this less than auspicious beginning more simulated attack profiles were flown, but the aircraft would flame out consistently when the stick was pushed forward to enter level flight. With this dangerous penchant, it obviously was unsuitable for combat. After much searching, the cause was traced to the fuel outlet's faulty vent system but the problem still remained to be solved. In spite of the setbacks, Luftwaffe High Command called for the structuring of the first operational unit of Me 163Bs (Fig. 7-1). By January 31, 1944 the first Staffel appeared on paper as a part of Luftflotte Reich's order of battle, and was labled 20th Staffel of Jagdgeschwader 1 (20./JG 1). Zwischenahn was listed as the base of operations and twelve Me 163s were assigned to the unit although neither crews nor aircraft existed.

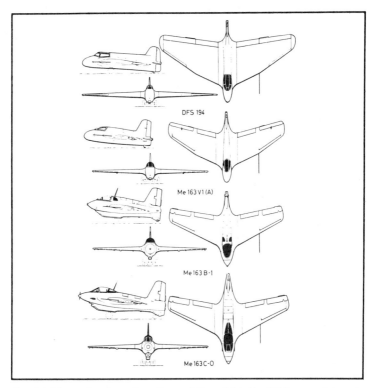

Fig. 7-1. These drawings show the evolution of the Me 163 from prototype to operational rocket fighter. A total of 364 were built, but less than one-fourth of those saw combat due to lack of fuel and/or pilots qualified to fly them. Komet production was ordered much too late for these craft to significantly affect the air war over Europe.

Captain Spate had been planning the deployment of the Komet ever since the beginning of 1943, envisioning them in large rings surrounding airfields in the west, northwest and north of Germany which lay under the path of Allied bombers penetrating the Reich. The fields would be within gliding distance of each other for rapid refueling and rearming and each would have its own radar facilities. The vision was never fulfilled as the Komet suffered still more agony in the hands of Luftwaffe planning specialists who placed the aircraft on only a few fields.

During February, 20./JG1 was redesignated 1./JG 400 under the command of Oblt. Robert Olejnik, who had joined EK 16 in November, after being Kommandeur of III Gruppe/JG 1. On March 1 Olejnik moved to Wittmundhafen with 12 pilots, although no aircraft were yet available to the Staffel.

o my Unit.

Good Omen

Later in the month Opitz delivered, to the new base, the first Me 163 to be armed with the 30mm Rheinmetall MK 108 cannon. Flying with rocket power from Zwischenahn, Rudy decided to give those below a dramatic first look at the Komet. Opitz dived vertically from 8,000 feet and, in his own words, "When I zeroed in on Olejnik's field for a high speed, low pass, long strings of tracer bullets came at me from all sides. With the engine shut down (no fuel remaining) I lived through some embarassing minutes. Somehow I outmaneuvered the fusillade and when I turned on final with flaps and skid down, the fire stopped and I could complete my landing without further interference. There were many apologies and embarrassed faces. We took it as a good omen that they had not achieved a single hit on the aircraft and smoothed things over at a roaring party at the club during which I was presented with a bottle of French cognac 100 years old."

In April, 2. Staffel/JG400 was formed on paper under Hptm. Otto Bohner, eventually transferring to Venlo in Holland. By May Erprobungskommando 16 was ready for actual fighter trials. On May 13, 1944 Spate had the Me 163BV41 fueled and armed for the rocket fighter's first combat sortie (Fig. 7-2). Without his knowledge the fighter had been painted a bright red by the mechanics in honor of Baron von Richthofen's Fokker Triplane.

At the first report of enemy aircraft Spate rose to intercept. He spotted two P-47s, and weaving tightly to avoid overtaking them too quickly, he accidentally let the stick slip out of his hand, causing an immediate flame out, 1,000 yards below and behind his quarry. During the two minutes required for a relight, he watched the P-47s all but disappear into the distance. Then, with a good restart, Spate brought the throttle into 3rd Stage to resume the pursuit. The Komet easily closed the distance — as the rearmost Thunderbolt filled his gunsight the indicated airspeed slipped part 550 mph. Without warning the Komet's left wing snapped down. Severe vibration set in. Instinctively Spate pulled back on the stick only to have the vibration increase. As the 163 bucked and yawed, negative G finally flamed out the engine and the shaking ceased. So intent on his quarry, Späte had encountered compressibility in level flight. He circled back to Zwischenahn for a safe landing.

Opitz made the next interception in the Me 163BV33 (GH+IN), encountering a twin engined reconnaissance aircraft (probably a Mosquito) over Zwischenahn, but the aircraft began to turn away before Rudy could gain enough altitude to give chase —

Fig. 7-2. Germany, first with the jet fighter, was also ahead of all other nations in the development of rocket power; not only with the V-2 missiles which began pounding London on 18 September 1944, but with introduction of the Messerschmitt 163 Komet rocket plane, which flew its first combat sortie in May, 1944.

the limited fuel supply of the 163 preventing a chase, similar to Späte's intercept. On May 20, 1944 Obfw. (Flight Sgt.) Nelte, an original EK 16 trainee, took off in the Me 163BV40 (Wk.Nr. 310049) in response to an Alarmstart (scramble) but he did not contact the enemy. These attempts were very premature but the armed Komets were ready and the pilots could not wait any longer to test the Komet's capabilities for the 8th Air Force was already pummeling the Reich heavily and its long ranging P-51 escorts were out to clear the skys of the Luftwaffe's fighter arm.

In the midst of these combat trials, another major blow against the Komet program was struck when Späte was transferred back to his old unit, JG 54, to lead its fourth Gruppe. Oberst (Colonel) Gordon Gollob, one of the Luftwaffe's most talented fighter pilots, (150 victories) was made type test leader, but he did not have the vision for the correct use of the Komet, a vision that had kept Späte working so hard to insure that the 163 was employed correctly.

Demonstration for the Brass

With full scale use of the Komet imminent, it was decided that a demonstration of the aircraft at Rechlin (the Luftwaffe proving grounds) for the Luftwaffe top brass and foreign dignitaries would benefit the 163 program. Pitz was ordered to make the flight.

Due to the haste in preparing for the demonstration, a new production 163B-1 was shipped to Rechlin without giving Opitz an opportunity to flight test the machine. When Opitz walked up to the aircraft for the first time he found out that it had not been flown at all since it came out of the factory! Since the machine had come from 1. Staffel there was also some hard feelings that no one from the unit was asked to fly the demonstration.

Regardless of the deteriorated situation, there was no canceling the Komet's portion of the Rechlin program. The flight was of great importance to the rocket fighter's future. Climbing into the aircraft, Pitz started the rocket engine and roared off down the runway with Göring and delegations of Japanese and Italians present to view what this revolutionary little rocket fighter could do.

At 13,000 feet Opitz throttled back to 1st Stage thrust, did a half loop and came out in inverted flight, rolling to avoid negative acceleration while initiating a dive for the field. At 300 feet Pitz rammed the throttle to 3rd Stage and made a maximum performance climb back up to 19,000 feet where the end of his fuel supply was signaled by a slight thump. After a few spirals, Rudy again put the Komet into a dive to gain speed, did a few aerobatic maneuvers down to 6,000, then dived again to whistle across the field, pulling up to make a 360° approach to the runway. During the last part of Pitz's program another of the show's participants, an Me 262 radioed for immediate permission to land due to low fuel. "I landed long," Opitz remembers, "to avoid any hazard to the jet following me and touched down on a narrow strip of turf alongside the hardtop runway. This strip was assigned to me prior to the flight. Apparently unknown to the authorities who assigned this strip for my landing, there was a zig-zag ditch running across it from the edge of the hardtop runway to a light anti-aircraft gun position on the edge of the field. This ditch loomed suddenly out of the fairly tall grass a very short distance ahead of me. My Komet had almost come to a complete stop when the skid dipped into that ditch. It caused the aircraft to rear up to a vertical position. There it remained for a second or two before it fell ever so gently on its back.

"I was not hurt, but firmly suspended, head down, by the pilot's harness. There was no immediate danger. Within seconds I was surrounded by soldiers from the nearby gun position who told me that they already saw rescue vehicles move out from the far side of the airfield. More out of curiosity than anything else, I asked them to try to get me out by digging a hole under the bubble canopy. This was done in minutes and I was already halfway out when the rescue vehicles arrived. Then suddenly, I saw a flame leap up in the rear corner of the cockpit. While I was pulled free I felt heat develop on my back and my glove covered left hand burst into flame.

"My life was spared only by the split second action of the rescue team which trained a fire hose on me and doused me completely with water, before all my clothes caught fire. Unknown to me, they had come in contact with traes of rocket fuel during my squeeze out of the cockpit. I came away with 3rd degree burns on my left hand but my back was uninjured.

"The investigators of the accident found an improperly installed fuel vent line responsible for the draining of a small amount of residual rocket fuel from the tanks into the cockpit after the Komet came to rest in an inverted position. We also learned from this accident that our prospective P.C. coveralls had serious drawbacks. While it was true that the P.C. material would not ignite when in contact with rocket fuel, it did not stop it from penetrating and then igniting normal clothing worn by the pilots below the coverall. When exposed to flame, as on my gloved left hand, it had the tendency to cake and then add to the seriousness of injuries caused by fire."

During May and June, 1 and 2 Staffel, at Wittmundhafen and Venlo, Holland, respectively, joined EK 16 in launching abortive interceptions against both single recon. aircraft and the American bomber formations. Each attempt met with failure but Allied pilots were beginning to come home with reports of strange tiny aircraft that climbed almost straight up at incredible speeds, marked by long contrails as they reached altitude. On May 31 a Spitfire recce pilot reported a "nearly all wing" aircraft come very close to intercepting him, then, without reason, disappeared. Obviously, it had either flamed out or run out of fuel.

By June 18, 1944 1./JG 400 had eleven Me 163Bs, five of which were operationally ready for combat. Before the month of July was over, Oberst Gollob had both Staffeln transferred to Brandis, near Leipzig. This was quite a blow to all concerned since Späte had worked so hard for dispersal of the Staffeln to Venlo, Deelen, Bad Zwischenahn, Wittmundhafen, Nordholz and Husum to implement his envisioned use of the Komet. Facilities had even been built at these fields but Gollob's ideas were formulated by his piston engine concepts of fighter superiority. He thought a concentration of the Komet's abilities at one field would be best. The pilots in particular were very disappointed with the choice since the field was far east of the enemy approach routes.

The massing of all Komets on one field meant sending them off two or three at a time at 20 second intervals, launching as many as possible in order to hit the bomber streams. This resulted in tremendous landing and servicing problems, since most of the Komets would also return in groups, due to their short endurance. Getting them off the field in time to avoid other landing aircraft was a virtual impossibility. This was further complicated by the 163's inability to "go around" during a landing approach . . . and the 163 could not taxi off of the field since it had to be towed by a small tractor (known by its brand name of Scheuschlepper — Shy Tug).

1. and 2. Staffeln coming together formed I Gruppe/JG 400/, under the command of Robert Olejnik, though the regulation three complete Staffeln per Gruppe was not followed. The Komet's mission was now officially described as Objektschutz-Jager (Target Interceptor), a designation that was to belong solely to the Me 163. In the case of Brandis the protected target was the Leuna synthetic fuel and rubber manufacturing complex, of crucial importance to the petroleum-starved German war machine.

As the personnel and aircraft came to Brandis in the last weeks of July, Olejnik wasted no time in setting up the Gruppe for combat operations, eagerly awaiting the opportunity to pit his Komets against the tremendous American air fleets. His opportunity came on July 28, 1944.

On this day the Eighth Air Force sent 569 B-17 Flying Fortresses to the Merseburg-Leuna complex with several fighter groups acting as escort. Below the long stream of American aircraft lay Brandis. JG 400 had Fw. Siegfried Schubert, Fw. Hartmut Ryll, Fw. Rolf "Bubi" Glogner, Lt. Hans Bott and three other rocket pilots sitting in their 163s on alert. The summer day was hot; canopies were open to gain some relief, as the Germans followed the progress of the "Dickie Auto", Fat Car (German slang for four engined bombers) by radio. As the bombers came into the IP Lt. Korff and the German ground controllers gave the JG 400 pilots orders for Alarmstart—oxygen masks were pulled on, hands up to signal the starter vehicle, controls tested, canopies slammed down, engines started and 3rd Stage thrust applied by the first two pilots. Just after the two Komets lifted off, three more made sharp starts, then the last two.

Missed Opportunity

At 0945 hours the 3rd and 4th Force bombers spotted the Komets coming straight up into the stream. 96th, 388th and 452nd Bomb Group personnel began to call out the positions of these strange projectiles that were climbing up to meet them. Arcing up above the formation, Schubert led the pilots back down into the stream, some diving through and between the bombers, coming out in the rear, others turning to engage the Mustang escort. Schubert was frustrated — the closing speeds had been far greater than he expected. Misjudgement caused all seven of the Komets to miss the opportunity of engaging the enemy.

Col. Avelin P. Tacon, Jr., CO of the 359th Fighter Group, had spotted JG 400 while furnishing escort for the B-17s at 25,000 feet with eight P-51s. "One of my pilots called in two contrails at 6 o'clock high and five miles back at 32,000 feet. I identified them immediately as jet-propelled aircraft. My section turned 180° back toward the enemy fighters, which included two with jets turned on and three in a glide without jets operating." The Komets and the Mustangs passed each other head on and Tacon estimated their speed at 500 to 600 mph. Taco initiated a split-S to latch on to them as they passed underneath but the 163s easily pulled away from the Mustangs — as Tacon pulled out of his maneuver one of the Komets was five miles away while the other had pulled up into the sun.

The July 28 encounter held surprises for both the Allies and the frustrated I Gruppe pilots. This was the first close encounter with either the rocket powered Me 163 or the turbo jet Me 262 . . . American P-51s, the finest allied fighters of the war, were suddenly obsolescent after this first run-in with "jet" aircraft (both the 163 and the 262 were referred to as jet powered by Allied pilots.)

The Komet pilots had all experienced flame-out difficulties this day, as they leveled off and negative acceleration shut the Walter engine off. Fortunately they were not in the immediate vicinity of American aircraft at that moment, but even this good fortune had a negative side. The old methods of ground control were still in use, since Späte's long sought after system of independent rocket fighter controllers never came into being. Thus, Komets were scrambled in the same manner used for the relatively slow climbing piston engined fighters and this placed the 163s far ahead of the enemy bombers in most cases. Too far! The instruments in the 163 were, for the most part, conventional, which resulted in spinning instruments that had to settle down for a few minutes before orders from the ground controllers could be followed.

Assuming that the rocket fighters were able to get within range of the American bombers, they encountered the disadvantages of fighting near Mach 1. Approach to the Allied formations was to be at 560 to 590 mph. Since the bomber stream would be traveling from 220 to 250 mph, this left an actual closing speed of about 340 mph or 500 feet per second when coming in from the rear. To open fire in excess of 650 to 800 yards was a waste of ammunition. Furthermore, the Komet had to disengage at 170 yards to avoid ramming. Closure from 650 to 0 yards was, therfore, accomplished in about four seconds, the last 200 yards or 1½ seconds being used for a climb over the enemy formation.

A head-on approach yielded about one second for the same procedure — one second to fire an effective burst! To add to the Quandary, the MK 108 cannon (with 60 r.p.g.) chosen for the heavy punch they delivered, were constantly jamming, a problem that was never solved. If they did not jam, they only put out a few rounds due to the relatively slow rate of fire (420 rounds per min.).

On July 29 the 1st and 3rd Air Divisions came back to Leuna. Six Komets were operational at Brandis. At 1145 hours Capt. Arthur J. Jeffrey, leading Newcross Yellow Flight of the 479th Fighter Group, spotted a single Komet making a pass on the crippled bomber they were protecting. Jeffrey and his wingman, 2nd Lt. Richard G. Simpson, shoved the throttles in their P-38s forward to catch the attacker. The Komet made two flight dives, then climbed, weaving, as Capt. Jeffrey closed in and opened fire. Strikes appeared on the 163. Climbing to 15,000 feet with intermittent bursts of power, the rocket fighter circled to the left. The Lightning managed to turn tighter, getting in a good deflection shot while closing to 300 yards.

The Messerschmitt performed a mild split-S and spiraled off into an 80° to 90° dive under power which Jeffrey followed, gradually easing out to 70° as he fired and observed strikes until the 163 began to pull away. Starting to pull out at 4,000 to 3,500 feet, indicating over 500 mph, Jeffrey finally managed to regain level flight at 1,500 feet under an overcast, blacking out momentarily. When he regained his vision the Lightning pilot could not find the Komet. Jeffrey would claim a probable but the Komet pilot got away. The 163 could pull out of a 90° dive with greater ease than a P-38 since the wing loading of the Komet was considerably less with empty fuel tanks.

Two days later, July 31, 1944, the order of battle for the Luftwaffe listed 1./JG 400 as having a total of 16 Komets, four operational, at Brandis. The previous two days of combat had already reduced operational effectiveness by two aircraft. 2. Staffel was still in the process of transferring to Brandis but two of its five Komets were operational. OKL had also given orders for a third Staffel, 3./JG 400, to be activated.

Komets were encountered on four different days in August 1944. Lt. Col. John B. Murphy and 1st Lt. Cyril W. Jones, Jr. of the 359th Fighter Group shot down the first "jet" claimed by the Allies as a definite kill. Protecting "Out-house Mouse", a 91st Bomb Group B-17, on August 16, both Mustang pilots pressed their attacks home on Lt. Hartmut Ryll. Several witnesses saw Ryll's Komet hit the ground.

Epic Encounter

Eight days later, on August 24, an epic encounter took place between the eight rocket fighters on alert at Brandis and a portion of the over 1,300 Fortresses and Liberators headed for Germany. Alarm-start was sounded at 1155.

The Komets were spotted by the 381st, 457th, 305th and 92nd Bomb Groups as the tiny fighters passed through 30,000 feet. Two 163s, one piloted by Fw. Siegfried Schubert, went on up to 36,100 before bringing power back. The controllers had put them a bit off the main stream so it was a bit difficult to spot the enemy. Descending back down to 19,700 Schubert sighted the Low Group, the 92nd, 1,600 feet above and relit his rocket, climbing to 5,000 feet above the bombers for an attack. It was just after noon and the B-17s were just entering the IP as the two Komets came ripping through the formation. Lt. Chester J. Pyska had seen the Komets rise for the attack and warned the Group to be ready. Schubert singled out the lead Fortress, flown by Lt. Koehler, closed in and registered strikes on the left wing, damaging it severely. The Fort staggered out to formation and never made it back to England. The Komet flashed by Koehler, low at 10 o'clock with his engine on, going under 1st Lt. Elvin E. Hendrickson's B-17.

The second 163, right behind his leader, came into the formation at 10 o'clock low and closed to 700 yards on 2nd Lt. Steve Nagy's Fortress, PY-R (42-31771). As the rocket fighter pressed home the attack in the few seconds available, firing one burst, Nagy's No. 4 engine caught fire and the "17" fell away from behind 1st Lt. Robert Swift's ship, spinning down to explode at 19,000 feet.

Another rotte came barreling through the formation and Lt. Swift was attacked for a full half minute as the Komets pressed to within 80 yards from 12 and 6 o'clock. 1st Lt. Harold H. Baird was attacked from the rear and below as a 163 made a single pass. The third 163 up intercepted 1st Lt. Lloyd G. Henry in JW-N at 25,000 feet. S/Sgt. Walter Maximuch, the tail gunner, watched the German press in from 7 o'clock slightly low, until the German was within 500 yards. The gunner caught the 163 with a direct burst — the Komet's tail was severely damaged. The 163 nosed over and dived straight down.

With rocket power on, Schubert had an unseen but very real enemy to contend with — exceeding critical Mach. Pulling the Komet back up into the sky above the enemy bombers, he brought everything under control and once again scanned the sky for possible targets. The 457th Bomb Group was just entering the IP for Weimar south of Leipzig—there were no German or American fighters near the group. Pointing his Komet back down into the stream, Schubert came in from 12 o'clock high at 1212 hours, singling out the No. 3 Fortress (42-97571) in the lead squadron, lead box, flown by Lt. Winfred Pugh. A few strikes registered on the Fort but the Komet pilot had to pass by and come in again for a rear attack. With a diminished rate of closure, Schubert's accuracy increased and strikes were made all over the right wing, the No. 4 engine being severely damaged. Pugh pulled out of formation at 25,000 feet after Schubert roared by, peeling off sharply into a spin. The B-17 seemed to pull out and then go into another spin until it exploded at 10 to 12,000 feet.

The 305th had been spectators all this time until the remaining *rotten* of rocket fighters attacked. The Low Group watched a Komet make two attacks, the first from 9 o'clock high and around, and out at 6 o'clock in a regular pursuit curve. The second attack was made from just slightly low at 7 o'clock, the Komet breaking away straight down after being fired on. Second Lt. E. Arnold, Jr., flying WF-P, was attacked from the tail slightly low. The 163 practically stalled as it neared the Fort, coming between the Low Group and Arnold's aircraft. The German peeled off slightly low toward 9 o'clock, then climbed above and made a second attack on the Low Group, closing in on 2nd Lt. P.M. Dabney in KY-A until strikes were registering all over the Fort. The Komet pulled away and zoomed out of sight as the Fortress went down and crashed.

Several more attacks were made on the 305th without significant results—the fierce combat had lasted longer than 15 minutes. During their last moments, the Komets were unable to catch two low flying B-17s due to cloud cover and lack of radar vectoring, for the radar center had already switched off its equipment thinking all of the 163s were down.

August 24 had been a murderous day for both the Eighth Air Force and I./JG 400. Had the rocket fighter pilots known that they downed twice the number of B-17s than they claimed, things might have looked a bit brighter. Three of their precious Komets had been destroyed versus two Fortresses, or so they thought. Schubert was not able to observe his first B-17 go down and Dabney in KY-A had not been seen to go down by the German pilots. Allied planners, however, were not slow to appreciate what could happen when the Komet pressed home its attack.

EK 16 was transferred to Brandis for weapons and engine testing. The training of new pilots became the responsibility of the newly formed Erganzungs Staffel of JG 400 under Olejnik. Opitz transferred with EK 16 to Brandis to take command of I. Gruppe. Not only was Rudy to bring the Gruppe up to full combat readiness but he was still responsible for training all 20 of the newly arrived pilots.

During five different days in September, JG 400 tangled with the American bomber fleets with some success. By October 3 orders came down for the formation of 3. and 4. Staffeln/JG 400 at Stargard near Stettin, on the Baltic.

On October 7, 1944 10 Komets were operational to face well over 1,000 bombers and fighters. Lt. Elmer A. Taylor, Willard G. Erfkamp and Everett N. Farrell of the 364th Fighter Group combined their skills to down a Komet. The German, while taking .50 caliber strikes, managed to evade his Mustang pursuers, but upon setting his Komet down in a field he was wounded as the P-51s strafed the aircraft. Numerous encounters took place with the bombers and two B-17s were thought to have been downed.

Oncoming winter weather slowed down combat operations for JG 400 but November 2, 1944 made up for much of the inactivity. As the Eighth Air Force's 3rd Air Division headed for Leuna, JG 400 began to respond. Their mission was to prove disastrous for the Komet pilots.

Lt. Bott was off. Then Strasnicki and Bollenrath took off as a Rotte, followed by Andreas and Golgner in the next Rotte. All five pilots came directly up into the bomber stream to tangle with the fighter escort as well as the bombers. Günther Andreas came in close enough to the rear of a Fortress to receive severe damage at the hands of its gunners. Breaking off he was jumped by Capt. Fred W. Glover who was leading the 4th Fighter Group. Flying a borrowed Mustang, he flamed the Komet but Andreas managed to bail out. Another 4th pilot, Capt. Louis H. Norley, shot down and killed Bollenrath. Strasnicki was listed as missing, the victim of the bombers' defensive fire power, and later found dead.

By this time Späte was back with JG 400 after some begging

myself. Rudy.
not true

Fighters. After his arrival he formed the Geschwader Stab (Fighter Wing Staff) to become Kommodore of the unit—it was not until this event that the unit was known as JG 400.

There were sporadic combat operations during the last fall days, but the weather caused Späte to call a halt to reassess the Komet situation. By January 1945 the Russian advance forced III. Gruppe, under Zeigler, to eventually return to Brandis. In February the OKL called a halt to 163 production. There were well over 100 brand new aircraft in the woods surrounding Brandis but not enough pilots or fuel to fly them. Less than 25% of the 364 Me 163s built ever saw combat .

✗ Opitz, who was commanding II. Gruppe at Stargard, was having great difficulty getting the unit fully operational in the face of the Russian advance. So confused was the situation, that all three staffeln were sent to three different fields, some not even suitable for flying the aircraft.

Combat operations continued to be sporadic. In February Späte disbanded the Geschwader Stab Schwarm, urging that resources be funneled to the Me 262. What was left of the Komet gruppen continued to fight as the opportunity arose but, again, without the advantages of a Geschwader organization. The word was out now to attempt interceptions primarily against reconnaissance aircraft.

March 15, 1945 was the last major encounter between the Eighth Air Force and the Me 163. Capt. Ray S. Wetmore of the 359th Fighter Group managed to down a Komet for his 22nd and last victory.

No Fuel, No Bases

By April the German Reich was a shambles. The Komet pilots had no fuel, no ground control, no advance warning of incoming enemy aircraft, no real bases. The two or three Komets that could be mustered by the mechanics at Brandis were boarded by the pilots who would simply sit and watch for contrails. Opitz had fully operational II. Gruppe at Husum but the unit's numerous moves had wreaked havoc on efficient use of the aircraft.

The sixth and last Allied kill over the Me 163 came on April 10, 1945 when F/O "Slops" Haslop, an Australian with 165 Squadron, RAF, shot down a Brandis based Komet with his Mustang III. All six Komet victories were made by Mustangs.

On April 20, 1945, the U.S. Army's 9th Armored Division rumbled into Fliegerhorst/Brandis finding most of the Komets

✗ my new Unit   Dec. 44

destroyed by the retreating Germans. II. Gruppe at Husum managed to down one Lancaster on April 22 when a single tank car of fuel got through.

Rudolf Opitz made the last powered flight in the Me 163 to test one of the aircraft that had flamed out during an April 22 mission. Starting procedure and take-off roll progressed without incident when suddenly, during rotation for lift-off, the fire warning light came on! A quick decision was imperative! It was too late to bring the 163 to a stop. A climb out at max power while pulling the fuel dump valve would eliminate the fuel load in the shortest possible time. It worked, but after the engine cut out the fire continued out of control. There was nothing to do but get out of the aircraft, something Rudy had never had to do with the Komet.

Pulling the emergency canopy release, Rudy watched the canopy move a few inches and stop—Rösle's flight all over again. Precious time clicked by before he was able to push the heavy canopy through the boundary layer of the air flowing around the 163, which was holding the canopy firmly in place. Sparks and T-Stoff fumes were then sucked forcibly into the cockpit, making vision extremely difficult.

The only alternative was a side-slip that was not too steep, since the air rushed in with screeching violence, tearing at the eyes, yet not too shallow so that the cockpit wouldn't clear. Rudy was able to spot Husum and with a few quick moves brought the Komet into a downwind leg for the field.

The Komet touched down on a rock-earth wall surrounding a field, just grazing it. The 163 sailed on and settled into the middle of a cow pasture with the ease of a feather. All looked good until the wall at the other end loomed up! Slithering across the meadow the careening rocket fighter slammed into the wall. The Fuselage with its armored nose went through as if the wall were paper, leaving the wings behind, then soared over a creek and onto the next field. Opitz, to this day, does not know how he got out of the 163 but he managed to warn a curious farmer to take cover and then crawl down into the creek just before the Komet exploded.

The crash crews found Rudy unconscious about 30 yards from the blanched pile of smoking metal that used to be his aircraft. Some of the trees surrounding the scene were on fire. Rudy was rushed to the hospital with several broken ribs, a broken collarbone and a broken arm.

—*Jeffrey L. Ethell*

I pulled him out to safety.

Chapter 8
Combat Flying the Focke-Wulf 190

Note: When we designed the Focke-Wulf Fw 190 in the summer of 1937, there were many in the Air Ministry who believed our fighter had little chance against the concepts then coming from Messerschmitt. But because we chose a radial engine that would not conflict with the short supply of liquid-cooled powerplants earmarked for aircraft then in production, yet one that promised a great deal more horsepower than available at the time, several of our friends in procurement persuaded the technical bureau to give our proposals a chance. By the summer of 1939, they were glad they had done so.

The Focke-Wulf 190 was designed to be built by a great number of small sub-assemblers. We designed it with ease of maintenance in mind, plus quick replacement of entire sections. It was a sturdy machine and extremely versatile. Although conceived as a fighter, it did double duty as an attack bomber and, in fact, throughout most of the war, was the only reliable, light attack bomber we possessed in numbers. In his review of the Fw 190 story, Robert Grinsell has given a true and accurate account."

—Kurt Tank □

Since the inception of manned flight, each decade of aircraft design has provided the world with a small and select group of functional, yet eye appealing fighter planes which not only survive the odds and action of the combat environment into which they are thrust, but also perform, over and above the demands made on them, with such dependability and flair that they are remembered long after their tours of duty have become history. The printed matter on these now famous fighters would fill a library, but in most instances the books and articles restrict their limited content to repetitive technical history and tend to ignore the aircraft's basic flying traits, weaknesses, advantages, and overall characteristics as seen through the eyes of the man who entrusted his very existence to it, the pilot. This story on the Focke-Wulf 190 will dwell on the design features and construction which formed the heart of this great aircraft, and on what the Fw was like to fly in combat against its counterparts, as recalled by one of the Luftwaffe's leading Fw 190 aces, Oskar Romm, who flew Fw 190 variants, from the A through the D, and who was credited with the destruction of 92 enemy planes in them.

Design History

The Focke-Wulf 190 was the result of a contract signed in the early autumn of 1937 between the German "Reichsluftfahrtministerium" (RLM) and Focke-Wulf for a single-seat attack and interceptor that was to be the successor to the Messerchmitt Me 109B, which at that time was just entering front line service with the Luftwaffe. The Chief Designer at Focke-Wulf, Dr. Kurt Tank, submitted several alternative concepts to the RLM during the first few months, the majority of which utilized the liquid cooled, in-line powerplant which was then in vogue due to its low frontal area and reduced drag characteristics. However, the one design Tank favored and the one for which he argued in depth was a radical configuration utilizing the powerful 14-cylinder air-cooled Bavarian Motor Works BMW 139 engine. Arguments in Tank's favor included the low susceptability of the powerplant to combat damage and the fact that the production and delivery schedules of the in-line liquid cooled engines for the Me 109 could be jeopardized by its use in another aircraft. Based on this data Tank was ordered to proceed with his new radial engined fighter, called the "Wuerger" (Butcherbird). The result of Tank's work provided the world with an extremely simple, compact, well-proportioned and highly streamlined aircraft which must be rated as one of the finest fighter planes of World War II.

Design Detail and Construction

The Focke-Wulf 190 offered the ultimate combination of simple, yet sturdy overall construction, housing highly complex subcomponents (Fig. 8-1). It was specifically designed from its inception for the pilot and the field maintenance man. What, at first inspection, appeared to be unnecessary complex, turned out to be a well thought out, tough, self-contained, and quickly removable component designed and suited for a specific purpose, each one included with the idea of reducing field maintenance time to a minimum. The Fw 190 was created on the philosophy that it is easier to get components replaced as a unit than to repair them. Therefore, the aircraft was also designed to be fabricated and

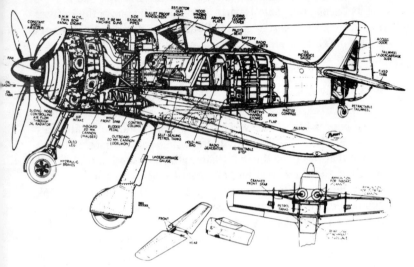

Fig. 8-1. Sectional view of the Fw 190.

assembled through a widespread network of subcontracting and dispersal plants. The fuselage, for example, was comprised of only two major components, the fore section extending from the firewall, or what the Luftwaffe called the No. 1 Bulkhead, to Bulkhead No. 8 aft of the pilot's seat, and the aft section which extended from Bulkhead No. 8 to the aft empennage.

The forward fuselage section was the heart of the plane and was, in effect, a double-deck box type structure, with the top section making up the pilot's cockpit and the lower section serving as the fuel bays. The firewall, or Bulkhead No. 1, was constructed of light sheet metal backed by sheet aluminum alloy riveted to flanges extending from the top two engine mount fittings down to a second set of fittings, which served as attach points for the lower side engine mounts and front wing spar.

Longerons ran aft from these four points to the No. 8 Bulkhead, where they were spliced to lighter supports in the aft section. The top longerons were 1-¾ inch wide U-sections made up of 3/16 inch aluminum alloy which also served as the tracks in which the cockpit canopy traveled. One stringer on each side, below the upper longerons, made up the only horizontal stiffeners in the upper portion of the fuselage. Aluminum alloy sheets riveted to the lower longerons, formed the cockpit floor, separating the pilot from the fuel bays.

One skin panel, attached to longitudinal and transverse angle shaped stiffeners, was attached to the lower fuselage section by nine screws along each side and five on each end, thus offering quick access to the two self-sealing fuel tanks which were suspended in the fuel bays with thick web fabric straps. On the upper fuselage section, immediately aft of the top engine mount fittings, the fuselage structure was flat, forming a shelf to which was bolted mounts for the 7.9 mm machine guns which were synchronized to fire through the propeller's arc (Fig. 8-2). Directly behind the gun mount shelf the fuselage extended to form the base for the windscreen, the front panel of which was 1-¾ inch bullet proof glass.

At the base of the front panel was the hinged fairing cover for the guns. This fairing, which hinged up and back for access to the guns and ammunition trays, was of waffle type construction, with a double skin being fastened together by a rivet in each inner skin dimple. Three heavy toggle locking switches were used on each side to hold the fairing in place. The heavy cowling, and easily removable hinges to keep it in place, added what appeared to be unnecessary weight. It was, however, in keeping with the apparent design theory. It was heavy enough to endure long hard wear and, as an added feature, the side panels swung downward around the engine mounts to be used as work platforms by the maintenance crew. Also, in case the cowling was bent, the toggles were sturdy enough to pull it into shape for quick locking and take-off. The

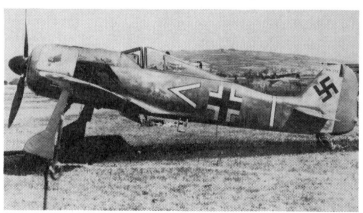

Fig. 8-2. A Focke-Wulf 190A-3, June, 1942; aircraft No. 313. Fast, well armored and heavily armed—four 20-mm cannon and two 7.9-mm machine guns—the Fw 190 was also fitted with a "Kommandgerat" or brain box that automatically adjusted fuel flow, mixture, propeller pitch and supercharger setting. Most Fw 190s were A-3 and A-4 models, the latter having a slightly modified fin and water injection.

cowling on the Fw 190 averaged 1.75 lb/sq-ft compared to the 1.25 lb/sq-ft for the typical British and American designs, and the Luftwaffe's persistent use of this cowling type through several model changes indicates their belief that the beating it could take and the speed with which it could be locked in place made it worth the added weight (Fig. 8-3).

The cockpit cover and its fairing were built as an integral unit. The base of the structure was of tubular construction bent into an inverted U at the front to fit the windscreen. The plexiglass of the canopy was mounted between strips of Buna rubber and a flat aluminum strip, and was held by screws driven into self-locking nuts in the tube. At the rear of the plexiglass was a stamped, flanged aluminum A-frame set between the tube-frame ends and riveted to an aluminum alloy fairing. The whole structure rode on three ball-bearing rollers, one on each side at the front of the plexiglass section in the top fuselage longerons, and one attached to the tube which ran in the channel section that was set in the fuselage turtle deck.

The canopy cover could be operated only from the inside by a crank attached to a sprocket which engaged a pin ratchet in the front end of the tubular frame. Emergency exit could be effected by pushing down on a small handle located near the crank. This disengaged the sprocket and then, through a series of rods and shafts, released a latch holding the firing pin. A cartridge was exploded and blew the rear end of the canopy backward far enough to let the slip stream get under it and pull it away. The explosive charge, about the size of a 12-gauge shotgun shell, was located aft of the armor plate in back of the pilot's head.

The radio antenna lead was fixed at the vertical fin and came over a pully series in the plexiglass just behind the armor plate. It

Fig. 8-3. Fw 190A-5/U-12. This variant was perceived as a "bomber destroyer," fitted with a pair of 20-mm cannon in a tray beneath each wing and 13-mm machine guns in the wing roots. Cowl guns were deleted.

then was run through another pulley series to the radio, mounted just behind Bulkhead No. 8. Regardless of the canopy position, open or closed, the antenna maintained the same tension.

The cockpit itself did not give the appearance of being over-crowded. Nevertheless, there was no wasted space. Flight and engine controls and indicators were arranged in two panels beneath the windscreen and on horizontal panels along each side of the pilot's seat. The seat, the back of which was made of steel armor plate, was only adjustable in a vertical attitude over a range of 4 inches and was designed for the use of seat-pack parachutes.

A departure from normal design contruction showed up in the Fw 190 wing. It was built as a single unit from tip to tip. Thus, if damaged structurally, any place between the detachable tips, the entire unit would be replaced. The integral center section of the tapering front spar was a very heavy member, for it took the weight of the two lower side and bottom engine mounts, fuselage fitting attachments, 20-mm cannon and main landing gear assemblies. At the centerline of the wing was a built-up, triple-web I-beam rein-forced by a heavy vertical channel shaped member containing, at its lower end, a forged fitting for the lower engine mount structure. Between the centerline and the side engine mounts were two vertical shaped stiffeners. Engine mount members themselves were of similar shape, but were heavier and were riveted rather than bolted to the main spar.

The fabric covered metal Frise-type ailerons were as light in weight as they were to control. They were built around a channel monospar with beaded verical stiffeners to which were riveted upper and lower two-layer metal leading edge skins, the inner ones having beaded stiffeners.

The main landing gear was a single-strut oleo shock unit with conventional torque scissors attached to a tapered roller bearing spindle assembly. The front face of the mounting was flanged to bolt to the front spar. The fairing was in three sections, one attached to brackets extending up from the hub, another bolted to the oleo strut and the third hinged at the center of the fuselage. A scale painted on the two fairings attached to the landing gear told at a glance if proper pressure, about 1300 psia, was being maintained in the shock unit (Fig. 8-4).

Retraction was electric, with a separate motor for each wheel. In the down position the oleo struts did not reach the perpendicular and there was no down lock on the gear. The two I-beams formed a straight line when the gear was down and this straight load,

Fig. 8-4. The Fw 190A-5/U-14 torpedo fighter with an enlarged fin and lengthened tailwheel strut was evolved to give punch to the Reich's limited aerial defense against sea forces. The "U" in this designation is for Umrust-Bausatze (factory conversion) thus, U-14 signifies the 14th such conversion.

coupled with the high reduction from the motor, was enough to prevent the gear from shifting from the down position.

Small metal contacts on the faces of the I-beam joints automatically shut off the motor when the gear was in the full down position. On the rotating member of the landing gear mechanism was a small scaled rod which projected up through a ball joint in the top of the wing as the gear went down so that the pilot could tell the exact position of the gear. The tail wheel assembly was attached by cables, which ran over the pulleys, to the main gear. It was automatically lowered and retracted in parallel with the main gear through this mechanical link.

The Fw 190's fuel supply, less the external drop tank, was carried in two self-sealing tanks suspended by fabric web straps in the lower fuselage section. The forward tank, between spars, held 61.2 gallons while the aft tank had a capacity of 76.8 gallons. Both tanks were filled from the right side of the fuselage, the filler pipe coverplates being quickly detachable flush units. Each tank contained a sealed electric pump. Gauges were all electric with the fuel warning light and pump indicator light being arranged vertically in the center of the lower instrument panel for easy recognition by the pilot.

Access to the Fw 190 was made via a retractable stirrup step provided on the left side of the plane. The stirrup was released by pressing a button near the top of the fuselage turtle deck. A hand-hold and a step, both covered by spring loaded panels, were also located in the left fuselage side.

Training and Combat in the Fw 190

Oskar Romm was born on December 18, 1919 in Haindorf, Czechoslavakia. A Sudetenland German, he joined the Luftwaffe in

October of 1939 and was sent to Muenchen/Freimann for six months of aircraft maintenance training and then to Pardubice, Pilsen and Bayreuth where he completed sixteen months of aircraft familiarization and flight training in various planes including the Focke-Wulf 44 "Stieglitz", Buecker "Jungman" and "Jungmeister", Focke-Wulf "Stoesser", and the Arado 56 and 59. In early 1942 he was posted to Kamenz, and Berlin/Werneuchen for advanced fighter training. From there he went to Krackau and Thorn in Poland where he received his final instruction on the Me 109.

"My training as a fighter pilot was completed on the Me 109 and progressed to completion without any problems. I became thoroughly familiar with this aircraft in every flying position and could hit gunnery targets with precise accuracy, but when I completed my training in the summer of 1942 I had two big surprises: (1) I was posted to JG 51 on the Russian Front and (2) I was informed that my future combat flying would be done in our new fighter, the Focke-Wulf 190.

"I arrived at JG 51's base in Russia in September 1942 and was immediately introduced to the Fw 190 through a series of technical lectures on its handling and flight characteristics. This was followed by actual flight training. The Fw 190 had a very compact form, an undercarriage with a wide track, and a very impressive armament with two machine guns and four cannon. It had a very characteristic and elegant streamlined cowl surface in which was housed a blower-cooled, 14-cylinder, double row radial engine, and this massive cowling defined for me the overall looks of this new fighter plane (Fig. 8-5).

"The arrangement and execution of the canopy offered excellent visibility. Within the cockpit I found a vast array of installed electric indicators and instruments. I recognized some old ones which had appeared in front of me in other aircraft, but I also noticed some new ones. These included the controls and instruments for the powerplant, propeller, armament, landing gear, flaps, and trim which were all located in a logical and easily visible layout.

"My first flying assignments were to make normal rounds of the field where I would shoot landings and then take-off again. More important, I was to learn to take off the Fw 190 from any position on the field, whether I was standing still or rolling along the runway after engine shutdown, and this knowledge would later save my life. As far as taking-off was concerned, you just pulled back on the stick, she lifted her "three legs" and away she went.

Fig. 8-5. An Fw 109A-4. Engine was the BMW 801D 14-cylinder two-row radial of 1,760 hp at 18,000 ft. Maximum speed was 395 mph at 17,000 ft. Normal gross weight was 8,580 lbs.

With the simple punching of buttons she retracted her gear and flaps, and provided trim. Her powerplant was unusually loud with a hard jarring sound, but with growing airspeed one lost the sense of the noise.

"To set her down, one just checked the rpms and, with a punch of a button, set the flaps to a lift position, then let the gear down. To turn into the final landing pattern and to trim the aircraft with the already extended flaps was a very simple matter. She would set herself down smartly and sure-footedly, almost landing herself, provided she had power. All flight maneuvers, including landing, presented no problems with this aircraft and as my training progressed my admiration for the Fw 190 grew.

"After completing the initial series of landings and take-offs I began training in two plane formation flying while practicing combat manuevers. This included strafing sorties and continuous gunnery practice. I became convinced that I could fly the Fw 190 as an armament platform with greater assurance and reliability under any and all conditions than I could the Me 109.

"She reacted quickly for her size to any and all my control commands. She was fast. She could climb. She could manuever with the best of her counterparts and she had an awesome battery of firepower. My instructor, an already accomplished front line combat pilot, would engage in mock aerial combat with me and once I mastered my controls he was never able to turn inside of me.

"My training continued with a specialized landing operation where we would land our Fw 190s from a very low formation, our goal being, that on our approach from any direction and while under possible enemy attack, we could set our aircraft down quickly and safely.

"As a fighter pilot in the first squadron, first group of Fighter Wing 51, I started my combat in the fall of 1942 from a field near Ljuban in the vicinity of Leningrad as number four man in a *schwarm* (flight) with the assignment of responsibility of "free hunting" in a given sector. We would fly in two and four plane formations looking for enemy aircraft to attack. Climbing to my assigned altitude on my first sortie I noticed that my oil temperature had exceeded the maximum allowable limit. (This was typical with this aircraft's powerplant during its early production.) I realized I could not make it back to our base so I cinched up my harness and set her down in a large open marsh area. On impact, my head and body lunged forward and I injured myself on the Revi C/12D reflector gunsight. The next day my nose looked like a large potato. Our maintenance crews dragged my plane from the swamp and it was sent to the repair depot. After my own recovery, I returned to Germany where I picked up a new Fw 190 and flew it back to our base in Russia. It was considered a matter of extra flight training time for me.

"A few days later I returned to combat status and began my second operational sortie with the Fw 190 from the unit's new base at Vyasma, south of Moscow. We encountered the formation of six armored Ilyushin Il-2 Stormaviks and immediately attacked. I destroyed one of the attack bombers but as I pulled out of my dive to seek out another target I saw, for the first time, a large fighter similar in design to my own Fw 190. It was a Lavochkin La-5 with a completely red cowl, which identified it as being from the Stalin Squadron. The Russian had me at a speed disadvantage and with this edge he went into a series of sweeping, climbing curves to get above me. I was also trying to gain altitude, but in tight spiralling turns, while my wingman provided me with underside protection. I received a radio call from our commander to reform with the flight, as we had exceeded our mission time and were being ordered back to our base. I dropped the chase, but before I pulled away I fired a burst at the Russian fighter as he flew through my six gun pattern. I saw no evidence of results as I banked over to reform with my wingman.

"I had now completed my first full combat sortie in the Fw 190 and although I had experienced an emergency landing in my initial effort, my faith in the fighter had increased. I had learned through my own experience that I must fly with greater precision and alertness and also I had learned the importance of height and speed in an aerial confrontation.

"In January 1943 I flew my third sortie as part of an escort formation for Ju 88s and He 111s. After the bombers had dropped their patterns, we turned homeward, but due to a low cloud bank were forced to fly at near ground level. Suddenly my plane started to vibrate violently. The Russian landscape became nothing but a blur. I was too low to parachute so I prepared to again crash land, something you tried to avoid in the 190 wtih a dead engine. Keeping my wheels up because of the deep snow, I skidded over the surface for more than two miles, before finally coming to a stop. I took the expensive clock from its panel and my signal pistol before climbing out, then I jumped into the snow and inspected the aircraft to see if I could determine what had caused my problems. I soon discovered that two of the three propeller blades were on a negative setting and that the hydraulic limiters or stops had been rendered inoperable in the Russian cold.

"From this time on I flew my Fw 190s with greater care and with greater attention to detail. I still had the will to push this machine to its limits and often times did. Shortly after this incident, I was called over by my crew chief to inspect an Fw 190 in which I had just completed a sortie. he showed me a series of "ripples" on the upper wing surfaces. I had flown home on "corrugated steel" as I had taken the wing skin beyond its design limits with some of my maneuvers. Only the incredibily tough steel main spar had held the wing together and saved the plane and, possibly me.

"From January 1943 on, the engagements in Russia became more difficult and I became more proficient in the handling of my machine. My third and fourth victories (two II-2s) were achieved with an attack on the engines and cockpit areas. (I liked to attack from the rear and slightly above to the side.) Both aircraft fell in flames only minutes after I initiated my attack. A third II-2 was destroyed on this mission by my commander, but in the engagement his Fw 190 came in contact with a tree. Even though his wing was severely damaged he managed to fly his plane home while receiving airspeed input from me, as his pitot tube had been left with the wing section in that tree. This was just another example of the fantastic ability of this aircraft to survive.

"From this time on I concentrated harder than ever on my gunnery and practiced until I felt I was shooting true. Thus I was able to gain my next six victories (II-2s) in a matter of only seven minutes.

"I only attacked Russian fighters such as the Lavochkin, Yakovlev, and Mikoyan when I had to secure our airspace from interception, when our fighter-bomber or bomber formations needed protection, or when the Russian fighters were serving as escort to Russian bomber formations which we were attacking. We no longer went up like we did during the "free hunts," specifically looking for enemy fighters.

"The time of massive and loose Russian formations was over, they were now flying in smaller, tighter and more mobile units. We began running into numerous Petlyakov Pe-2 fighter-bombers in this new type of formation and against this aircraft I had great success. Short bursts into the powerplants of this machine almost certainly resulted in immediate and rapid burning or explosions.

"After gaining my 70th victory in the Fw 190 I was relieved of combat duty and sent to Toulouse, France as an instructor, returning to JG 51 in February 1944. Then in May, 1944, I was assigned to IV/JG 3 as part of the controversial *"Abshuss oder Rammen"* (Victory by ramming). This unit was flying specially specially modified Fw 190s with increased armament and armor protection around the pilot and powerplane. They were to be used for interception and destruction, by ramming if necessary, of the American bomber streams then ranging far inside Germany.

"On July 7th I flew my first sortie with this unit and the heavier Fw 190 A-8 against a tight formation of Consolidated B-24 Liberators. I searched out a bomber and from very close range, I poured short burst into the fuselage and the starboard engines. The impact of our new, improved 20 mm shells was devasting. The crippled B-24J immediately lost altitude and sheet metal as it began to burn, the aircraft exploding as I completed my overflight. I watched as the wing split away from the fuselage, the powerplants spinning off the wing like Olympic torches. I had also received some hits from the bomber during the attack, both in the engine and fuselage, but the heavily armored Fw 190 just kept flying.

"My next sortie was against a formation of Boeing B-17Gs and their P-51 Mustang escort fighters. To draw off the escort we would set up "fighter traps" in the sky and these would develop into an aerial circus. (In the ensuing, twisting melees everyone would be shooting; sometimes even at the enemy.) I came so close to one of the Mustangs that I could observe the squadron or personal marking of a "sea-horse" on his nose.

"On September 27th and 28th I accounted for five more American bombers during a pair of missions, (three B-24s and two B-17s). But when I returned from the latter mission I found that our field was under attack from a flight of red-nosed Mustangs and the special emergency landing procedures we had practiced in the summer of 1942 paid off as I set my Fw 190 down safely among the machine gun bursts and pock marks on the strip. I jumped from my cockpit to the wing and from the wing to the ground. As I hit the earth my legs buckled slightly and I ended up on my knees. Suddenly, I felt a sharp pain race through my knee and reached down with my hand assuming I had been shot. But I only came up with and old horseshoe, which I had always felt was a good luck symbol.

"At about this time in the war the Luftwaffe fighters of the "Home Defense" (of which JG 3 was a part) were being criticized by people at home who did not know the true field situation of over-powering odds, short supplies and almost constant alert. We often flew 5 or 6 sorties per day in summer. We were accused of cowardice in the face of the enemy and court martials were mounted by some officers in an effort to quiet the situation. I defended eight of my comrades in these proceedings and got them acquitted, for they were truly innocent.

"In January 1945 the badly depleted IV Gruppe of JG 3 was regrouping and I was given command of the 15th Staffel. We flew fighter-bomber sorties in our Fw 190s against the heavy armor and advancing convoys of the Soviet Army. My 190 performed beauti-fully in her new role. Based just a few kilometers from the front, we flew in at low altitudes in a loose formation carrying bombs with delayed fuses. We would drop our load at less than 300 ft. And then bank up and out to get out of range of the impending explosion.

"In February 1945 we moved to Prenzlau near Berlin and I was given full command of IV Gruppe. My command flight received the new Focke-Wulf Fw 190D-9 which was, and is, the fastest prop driven aircraft I have ever flown. It was supplied with a gyro-stabilized Revi 16b reflector gunsight and with this sight I found I could hit the cockpit of a Russian DB-7 twin engined bomber from a very great distance. The Fw 190D-9 included all the good qualities of the regular Fw 190 with a higher speed and a higher climb rate. It also included a water-methanol (MW 50) injection system that not only boosted power output, but also reduced engine temperatures under high rpm situations.

"I accounted for my final aerial victories in the Fw 190D-9 before ending my fighting career on April 24, 1945. On this day I was flying against the warnings of my Geschwader Kommodore who insisted I reduce my flying time. I got into an engagement with a formation of Il-2s and just as one of the enemy planes entered my sights I noticed my cooling manifold doors come open, my instruments registering overheating. I broke off my attack and luckily managed to elude the Russian fighter escorts. But by the time I was free of the battle I had lost too much altitude to parachute. Suddenly the engine quit and I tightened my harness and prepared for the inevitable. The Fw 190D-9 dropped like a rock into an open field and proceeded to smear its pieces all over the landscape. However, the same rugged construction that had saved my life in earlier emergency landings proved itself once again, although the injuries I did receive from the crash kept me from returning to active combat before the war came to an end.

"I began and ended my combat flying in the Focke-Wulf 190, and on both the first and last sorties, found myself sitting in the rugged cockpit after an emergency landing. However, between these two particular events, a span of over two and half years of almost continuous aerial fighting against increasing odds, resulted a very strong and affectionate bond between myself and this aircraft. I feel, as I am sure most combat pilots who flew a given model aircraft for the war's duration do, that my plane, the Fw 190, was the finest all around fighter of the war. She never let me down when I needed that little something extra and I owe both my victories and my life to this splendid machine."

—Bob Grinsell

Chapter 9
The Best Of The Breed

Note: Anyone who believes that he can satisfactorily demonstrate which WW II fighter was "best" out of the whole bag that appeared from 1940 to 1945 is incredibly naive. There are so many performance variables and kinds of missions, that arguing them all to a bedrock conclusion that would convince everyone is virtually impossible. There were a few generally acknowledged leaders, however, fighters which became household words the world over. The Spitfire, Mustang, Thunderbolt and Focke Wulf 190 all proved themselves in the crucible of war. The Me-262 was the first operational jet fighter and a dazzling achievement, years ahead of anything we had. But another household word, the highly propagandized ME-109G, was obsolete when it was built and was aerodynamically the most inefficient fighter of its time. It was a hopeless collection of lumps, bumps, stiff controls, and placed its pilot in a cramped, squarish cockpit with poor visibility.

Putting aside the relative merits of one fighter versus another, there was a simple truth that quickly emerged from your first engagement with the enemy: Whichever one of you saw the other one first had the winning advantage.

The most subjective variable is the experience and ability of the pilots. Their state of training was certainly an essential factor. Thus Clair Chennault was able to recruit experienced Army and Navy reserve pilots and civilians with a solid log book into the AVG "Flying Tigers", who flew for China in 1941, and chalk up a 12 to 1 victory loss ratio with P-40s. The ultimate measure of combat effectiveness in fighter operations is the victory-to-loss ratio and there are several factors in the equation that one can juggle if necessary, but you deal yourself all the high cards that you can. That's another way of saying that unless you were willing to close with the enemy in decisive combat, using all the advantages that you have, and carve your initials on him, then your government made a mistake in pinning those wings on you.

So I must leave it to the reader to conjecture about pilots and crews while we talk about airplanes. What follows is intended to give the average aviation enthusiast some idea of how the fighters in Europe compared with each other in performance and maneuverability. The data on British and German aircraft come from the Royal Aircraft Establishment, Farnborough. Data on the American fighters come from the National Advisory Committee for Aeronautics test reports and, in addition, figures on the Mustang have been verified by data from North American Aviation flight test reports where it was possible to do so. □

The first German aircraft that was shot down over England and which landed intact was a Heinkel 111 brought down on 28 October 1939. Two of the four crew were dead but the airplane survived in one piece except for a few bullet holes. A Ju 88 was shot down a few days before, but it crashed into the sea, a total loss. As the war went on into 1940 and the Battle of Britain was engaged, German aircraft fell all over England. Different types were quickly recovered in various stages of disrepair and subsequently arrived at experimental stations for analysis and to be made flyable again, if possible. Those that were brought down by fighers of anti-aircraft guns were usually basket cases. The more favored carcasses were those that landed because of engine failure, exhausted fuel or bad navigation. Abundantly provided by these sources, the British soon had a "flying circus" of captured German aircraft with RAF markings that toured the air bases in Britain to allow familiarization of new crews with the armament, performance and weaknesses of the opposition.

The idea of building a fighter to meet every performance requirement is out of the question. At best, each design is a compromise with priority emphasis on one or two qualities. Thus the Spitfire was a true interceptor designed primarily for the

Fig. 9-1. The Supermarine Spitfire Mk IX was Britian's answer to the Fw 190. It was probably the best point defense interceptor of the war. In its later models, such as the Griffon-powered Spit 14, there was no better sprinter. It out-climbed everything to 44,000 ft, was the ultimate in maneuverability.

defense of the British Isles, a sprint climber with a small turning radius (Fig. 9-1). The Mustang, after its conversion to the Merlin engine in 1942, was a fast, long range, strategic escort fighter with an easy 8-hour endurance. Like the T-bolt it would dive like a banshee, well ahead of the Spit and all German craft. However, in rate of climb the Me-109G was 200-500 feet per minute ahead of the Mustang up to 20,000 feet, then the '51 pulled ahead on up to 40,000 feet, while the Spit Fourteen would climb faster than any of them at any altitude from sea level up.

Generalizations in narrative form are difficult to make and by the time you get to the end, the conclusions are so fogged up the reader can't tell where he's at. We will, therefore, deal primarily in numbers of two kinds — One group is those that are measured against time: speed, endurance, rate of climb and acceleration in a dive. The second kind is those that are measured by distance: range and turning radius. Speed, most emphatically, was not everything.

Before we get into the performance comparison competition, some acquaintance with the features of the aircraft that we're talking about is necessary for the understanding of why things turned out as they did. If you're handy with a slide rule you can do your own mission profiles and performance variations. Data are also presented on the Me-110 and the Ju-88 because they were classed by Germans in a dual role, as fighters and as bombers. The latter in fact had a universal classification as a fighter, bomber and dive bomber and it sported dive brakes and an "Automatic Pull Out" feature that we'll also look at.

ME-109

The characteristics of two ME-109 models are of historical interest, the "E" and the "G". The E formed the backbone of German fighter strength during the Battle of Britain, its opposition being the Spitfire I and the Hurricane I. The G was the prevailing type in 1944 during the Battle of Europe and its main opponents were the Spit Fourteen, the Thunderbolt and the Mustang. So it is worthwhile to explore more fully the characteristics of the ME/109 because it was the longest lived of fighters produced in Germany and because it was the most highly propagandized. While it was a worthy opponent in 1939 it was outclassed by 1942; by 1944 it was manifestly obsolete ((Fig. 9-2).

An intact Me-109E with wing cannon was captured by the French in the summer of 1940 and was flown to England for flight test and evaluation. There were three stages of development prior to the G. First was an early version of the 109 flying in 1938 with a 670 hp Jumo 210 engine, a fixed pitch wooden prop and two synchronized guns. Second was a variable pitch two-bladed prop model and the addition of two wing guns. Third was the E model, with a far more powerful engine, the DB601, which was an inverted V-12 of 1100 hp with direct fuel injection driving a 3-blade variable pitch prop. Its wing structure was beefed up, but in the process of "designing" in additional engine and structural weight, the engineers screwed up the center of gravity, and 60 pounds of permanent ballast had to be added to the rear of the fuselage to get the C.G. back. As a pilot and an engineer I can only be sympathetic the 109 pilots. Who needs that kind of millstone around his neck in a fighter? Pilots had nothing to say about the design faults of airplanes in Germany. They had damn little to say about them in England or in this country, at that time. Designers didn't have to fly their mistakes; they just produced them. Most of them didn't know how to fly and didn't want to learn, but more about that later.

In size, the Me-109, all models, was the smallest fighter produced by Germany or the Allies. That gave it a high wing loading for that time, about 32 lb./sq. ft. for the E. The Spit I and the Hurricane I were about 25 lb/sq. ft. at their normal combat weight. The 109-G was about 38 lb/sq. ft. as compared to 35 lbs. for the P-51B.

Fig. 9-2. Overworked, over-publicized and oftern overrated, the Messerschmitt 109 was actually obsolescent by 1942. Necessity and an excellent engine stretched its operational life.

	ME-109E	ME-109G
Mean weight, lbs.	5580	6450
Engine	DB 601	DB 605A
Horsepower	1100/15,000 ft.	1475/22,000 ft.
Power loading, lbs./HP	5.07	4.37
Wing loading, lbs./sq. ft.	32.1	37.5
Prop. diameter, ft.	10.2	9.83
Gear Ratio	14/9	16.85/10

Wing Geometry:

	ME-109E	ME-109G
Area, sq. ft.	174	172
Span, ft.	32.4	32.6
Mean Chord, Ft.	5.36	5.38
Aspect Ratio	6.05	6.10
Dihedral degrees	5.75	"
Sweepback, degrees	1.0	"
Root chord, ft.	7.03	7.0
Tip chord, ft.	3.42	"
Root thicknesses, percent chord	14.8	14.2
Tip thickness, percent chord	10.5	11.3
Slat length/span, percent Slat Chord/local chord, percent	11.8	Approx. same
Wing Twist, Root to tip	0	0
Speed, mph	354/12,500 ft.	387/23,000 ft

The fastest "G" subtype was the G-10 capable of 344 inch at S1 or 428 mph at 24,000 ft, with a meager range of 350 miles and an endurance of 55 minutes, but it wasn't introduced until the spring of 1944. Too little, too late, and still lacking in range and endurance.

Engine and Propeller. In principle, the DB601 and 605 series engines were the same as the Allison or Merlin, except they were inverted and had direct fuel injection; otherwise they were 12 cylinder, 60 degree Vee, glycol cooled engines. The prop was a 10.2 foot, 3 blade variable pitch mechanism of VDM design. Here is another major difference between their design approach and ours. The pitch on the ME-109 prop could be set at any value between 22.5 and 90 degrees, a visual pitch indicator being provided for the pilot. There was no provision for automatically governing the rpm. We did just the opposite, using a constant speed governor and flying by a constant tachometer indication of rpm. For any flight condition the rpm remained constant. We did not know, or care, what the blade angle setting was.

Wings and Controls. The wings had straight leading and trailing edge taper and no geometric twist from root to tip. The airfoil section had a 2 percent camber with the maximum thickness at the 30% chord position. The E thickness ratio was 14.8 percent at the root and 10.5 percent at the tip. All of that was standard design practice for the mid-1930s. What was new for fighter design was the leading edge slats which ran 46% of the span. There was no damping device fitted to the slat mechanism, they'd bang open at 120 mph with the airplane clean or at 100 mph with gear and flaps down. Each control surface was mass balanced. Another unusual feature was that as the flaps were lowered, the ailerons automatically dropped, coming down 11 degrees for the full flap movement of 42 degrees.

There were no movable trim tab controls on the ailerons or rudder, although both had fixed tabs that could be bent on the ground. Pitch trim was affected by changing the stabilizer incidence through a range of 12 degrees. The design scheme was that both the flaps and the stabilizer were coordinated mechanically from two 12 inch wheels mounted concentrically on the left side of the pilot's seat. By twirling both wheels in the same direction the pilot could automatically compensate for the change of pitch trim due to lowering or raising the flaps. Differential coordination could be set by moving one wheel relative to the other.

Performance Evaluation. The first surprise you would get in planning a test hop with the Me 109 is that you're limited to about an hour with some aerobatics at combat power, because the internal fuel capacity is only 88 gallons; with a drop tank, the "G" carried a total of 154 gallons. I'll never understand why the fuel capacity designed in Luftwaffe fighters was so limited. It was a major design deficiency that contributed to their loss of the air war, but even more puzzling is the fact that it could have been quickly changed for the better anytime from 1940 onward, but it wasn't.

Takeoff was best done with 30 degrees of flaps. The throttle could be opened quickly without loading or choking up the engine. In fact, the Daimler Benz engine was the best thing about that airplane. The stick had to be held hard forward to get the tail up, and it was advisable to let the airplane fly itself off. If it was pulled off at low speed the left would not respond and on applying aileron the wing would lift and fall again with the aileron snatching a little. If no attempt was made to pull it off quickly, the takeoff run was short and the initial climb good.

The absence of a rudder trim control in the cockpit was a bad feature at speeds above cruise or in dives. Above 300 mph the pilot needed a very heavy foot on the port rudder pedal for trimmed flight with no sideslip which is absolutely essential for gunnery.

The pilot's left leg quickly tired while keeping this load on, and this affected his ability to put on more left rudder for a turn at 300 mph or above. *Consequently, at high speeds, the 109 could turn far more readily to the right than to the left.*

A series of mock dogfights were conducted by the British in addition to the flight tests and the following was revealed:

Dives. If the airplane was trimmed for level flight, a heavy push on the stick was needed to hold it in a dive at 400 mph. If it was trimmed into the dive, recovery was difficult unless the trim wheel was wound back, due to the excessive heaviness of the elevator forces.

Ailerons. At low speeds, the ailerons control was good, response brisk. As speed increased the ailerons became too heavy but the response was good up to 200 mph. Between 200 mph and 300 mph they became "unpleasant". Over 300 mph they became impossible. At 400 mph the stick felt like it was set in a bucket of cement. A pilot exerting all his strength could not apply more than one fifth aileron at 400 mph; that's 5 degrees up and 3 degrees down. The aileron situation at high combat speeds might be summarized in the following way:

1. Due to the cramped cockpit a pilot could only apply about 40 pounds side force on the stick as compared to 60 pounds or more possible if he had more elbow room.

2. Messerschmitt also penalized the pilot by designing in an unusually small stick top travel of plus or minus 4 inches, giving very poor mechanical advantage between pilot and aileron.

3. At 400 mph with 40 pounds side force and *only* one fifth aileron displaced, it required 4 seconds to get into a 45 degree roll or bank. That immediately classifies the airplane as being unmaneuverable and *unacceptable as a fighter*.

Elevator. This was a good control at low speeds but became too heavy above 250 mph and at 400 mph it became so heavy that maneuverability became seriously restricted. When diving at 400 mph a pilot, pulling very hard could not pull enough "g" force to black himself out. The stick force per "g" was in excess of 20 pounds in a high speed dive. To black out, as a limit to the human factor in high speed maneuvers, would require over 100 pounds of pull on the stick.

Rudder. At low speeds the rudder was light but sluggish in response. At 200 mph the sluggishness disappears, at 300 mph the absence of a trim control in the cockpit became an acute problem.

The pilot's leg force on the port rudder above 300 mph to prevent sideslip became excessive and unacceptable.

Control Harmony. At low speeds, below 250 mph, control harmony was good, only a little spoiled by the sluggishness of the rudder. At higher speeds the aileron and elevator forces were so high that the word "harmony" is inappropriate.

Acrobatics. Not easy to do. Loops had to be started from about 280 mph when the elevator forces were getting unduly heavy; there was also a tendency for the wing slats to bang open at the top of the loop, resulting in aileron snatch and loss of direction.

Below 250 mph the airplane would roll quickly but there was a strong tendency for the nose to fall through the horizon in the last half of the roll and the stick had to be moved well back to keep the nose up.

Upward rolls were difficult, again because of elevator heaviness at the required starting speed. Due to this, only a moderate pull out from a dive to build up speed was possible and considerable speed was lost before the upward roll could be started.

The very bad maneuverability at high speeds of the ME-109 quickly became known to the RAF pilots in 1940. On many occasions 109 pilots were led to self destruction when on the tail of a Hurricane of Spitfire at moderate or low altitudes. The RAF pilot would do a snappy half roll and "split ess" pull out, from say 3,000 feet. In the heat and confusion of the moment the 109 pilot would follow, only to discover that he didn't have enough altitude to recover due to his heavy elevator forces and go straight into the ground or the Channel without a shot being fired.

Turning Radius. At full throttle, at 12,000 feet, the minimum turning radius without loss of altitude was about 890 feet for the Me-109E with its wing loading of 32 pounds per square foot. The corresponding figure for the Spit I or Hurricane was about 690 feet with a wing loading of 25 pounds.

While the 109 may have been a worthy opponent in the Spanish Civil War or during the Battle of France in early 1940, it became a marginal airplane against the Spits during the attack on Britain in September of that year. By 1942, even with the appearance of the "G," it was definitely obsolete. However, the Germans continued to produce it as the backbone of the Luftwaffe fighter forces. The attitude of the Nazi high command was that this was going to be a quick "blitz" war and if they lost three 109s for every Spitfire shot down, that was acceptable. In fact, in 1940 the official policy was laid down that the development of all aircraft types requiring more than 6 months for completion was prohibited. They'd turn out the existing designs like hot cakes and swamp the RAF with production.

That doesn't say much for any charitable concern they should have had for the unnecessary loss of pilots caused by going into combat with a substandard airplane. But, after all, no one has ever said that the Fuehrer and Goering had any anxiety about their pilots or troops. Quite the contrary, the record of history shows that they had none.

Furthermore, no designer in that period would pretend that he could stretch the combat effectiveness of a fighter for 7 years, 1935 to 1942, without *major* changes in power plant or aerodynamics, or, better yet, going to a new design. Technology in design in that era was changing too fast. The reader might well say, "The Spitfire was certainly a long line of fighters, about 10 years, how come?"

The Spitfire was an aerodynamically clean airplane to start with, having a total drag coefficient of .021 at cruise. The Me-109 had a coefficient of .036; drag coefficients are the measure of an airplane's efficiency and of the horsepower required to haul 'em around. Like golf scores, the lower the better, and no fudging.

The British, in particular the staff at Vickers Supermarine, had done their homework in aerodynamics and put out a clean airplane that had the potential of longevity and increased performance. They had only to wait for Rolls-Royce to pump up the horsepower on the Merlin, which they did, by going from 790 hp in 1934 to well over 2,000 by 1945. The Merlin, in my opinion, was the best achievement in mechanical engineering in the first half of this century.

Messerschmitt practically ignored the subject of low drag aerodynamics and one can tell that by an inspection of the 109E or G. The fact is evident even in close-up photographs. *It was aerodynamically the most inefficient fighter of its time.* That's a puzzling thing when one realizes that much of the original work on high speed drag and turbulent surface friction was done in Germany in the 20s and 30s. Messerschmitt was surrounded by it. Further, the work in England and the U.S. in this field was in the open literature, at least until 1938.

I also suspect, again from the record of history, that Willy Messerschmitt was too busy becoming a *Direktor* of Messerschmitt A.G. to concentrate on improving his status as an *ingenieur*.

Having gone this far, let me carry this affront to Messerschmitt's engineering reputation one step further.

An airplane factory can get things done awfully fast, in any country and in any language, once the engineers and sheet metal benders understand what is wanted. Every factory has a "development shop" or its equivalent, which is a full scale model or prototype shop with 100 or 200 old pros in every skill. Having that many coffeedrinkers, pipe smokers and "yarn spinners" around on the payroll, let's clobber 'em with a bundle of shop drawings on a clean up of the ME-109. Object: to make it a 400 mph plus airplane. Time . . . 30 days. The information and techniques required are currently available as of 1940. It's all written up in unclassified reports.

1. Cancel the camouflage paint and go to smooth bare metal. Besides the weight, about 50 pounds, the grain size is too large when it dries and it causes turbulent friction over the entire airplane surface. That may take a phone call to the brass. They're emotional about paint jobs. "Image," you know.

2. Modify the cockpit canopy. Remove the inverted bathtub that's on there now and modify as necessary to fit the ME-209-VI canopy. That's the airplane that set the world speed record in 1939.

3. Get rid of the wing slats. Lock them closed and hand fit a strip, upper and lower surface, that will close the sheet metal gaps between the slat and wing structure. That gap causes the outboard 15 feet of each wing to be totally turbulent.

4. As aerodynamic compensation for locking the slats, set up jigs and fixtures on the assembly line to put in 2 degrees of geometric twist from root to tip, known as "washout."

5. Modify coolant scoop inlet fairings. The square corners that are there now induce an unnecessary amount of drag. Also lower inlet 1 to 2 inches below wing surface to get it out of the turbulence of the wing surface.

6. Install complete wheel well fairings that cover the openings after the gear is retracted.

7. Retract tail wheel.

All of the above could have been done in 30 days but it wasn't. I don't know why. Someone would have to ask Willy . . . it's for him to say.

Fw-190A

A superb airplane, every inch a fighter. It could do a half roll at cruising speed in *one second*. Taking this in conjunction with the airplane's high top speed and rate of climb one expected its pilots to exploit its high speed qualities to the fullest without staying in there to "mix it up" in a low speed, flaps down full throttle, gut wrenching dog fight.

They did. The 190 pilots had a good airplane and some good advice. Nearly all of my encounters with the 190 were at high speeds. On at least two occasions when I met them, my Mustang started porpoising, which means I was into compressibility, probably around 550 mph. I don't know what my air speed indicator was reading, I wasn't watching it.

On another occasion, I jumped one directly over the city of Paris and fired all my ammo, but he was only smoking heavily after a long chase over the town. Assuming I was getting 10 percent hits, that airplane must have had 200 holes in it. It was a rugged machine.

Mean weight, lbs.	8580
Engine	BMW 801D
Horsepower	1600
Power loading, lbs./HP	5.36
Wing loading, lbs./sq. ft.	41.7
Prop. diameter, ft.	10.86
Wing Geometry	
Area, sq. ft.	205
Span, ft.	34.5
Mean chord, ft.	5.95
Aspect Ratio	5.8
Dihedral, degrees	5
Sweepback, degrees	5.5
Root chord, ft.	7.45
Tip chord, ft.	4.05
Thickness Ratio, percent	12
Max. thickness location	Between 25 and 30 percent
Top speed, mph	408/20,600 ft.

Fig. 9-3. The Focke-Wulf 190 was, without doubt, the best Luftwaffe prop-driven fighter built in significant number. Versatile and dependable, its biggest fault was in the positioning of its oil tank, engine-cooling fan and circular oil cooler, ahead of the engine, where all three components were vulnerable to gunfire.

Engine and Propeller. The BMW 801D was a 14 cylinder, twin row radial with direct fuel injection. A 10.9 foot diameter, 3-bladed VDM prop was used and was provided with hand lever or automatic pitch control. The 801D radial air cooled engine first appeared on the Dornier 217 and the FW-190. Its most novel feature was the geared cooling fan which ran at 1.7 times the crankshaft speed. A second feature was the oil cooler system which was a number of finned tubes shaped into a ring of tubes a little larger in diameter than the cooling fan. This ring was fitted into the rounded front portion of the cowling just aft of the fan.

I don't think this was such a good idea. For example, my principal aiming point was always the forward portion of an enemy ship; the engine, cockpit, wing root section. If you get any hits at all, even only a few, you're bound to put one or two slugs into the engine compartment. Having a couple of bullets ricochet off the engine block and tear up some ignition harness is not too bad, at least not fatal. But to have all those thin-walled oil cooling tubes *ahead* of the engine is bad news. Any hits or ricochets in the engine section are bound to puncture the oil tubes. Then the whole engine is immersed in oil spray, and sometimes it would flash over into a fire (Fig. 9-3). All of the 12 Focke Wulfs that I shot down sent off a trail of dense, boiling oil smoke heavy enough to fog up my gun camera lens and windshield if I were so close.

Wings and Controls. Again, as in the case of the ME-109, no trim tabs adjustable in flight from the cockpit were provided for the aileron and rudder. European designers seem to have acquired the notion that this was a nuisance or unnecessary. Not at all; when going into a dive, it's very easy for the pilot to reach down with his left hand and flick in a couple of half turns of rudder trim. It's not only desirable but necessary to eliminate side slip for good gunnery. The FW 190, however, did have electric trim tabs for the elevators.

Performance Evaluation. The FW 190's handling qualities were generally excellent. The most impressive feature was the aileron control at high speeds. Stick force per "g" was about 9 pounds up to 300 mph rising to 12 pounds at 400 mph as compared to over 20 pounds for the Me-109.

High speed stalls under "g" load were a little vicious and could be a fatal handicap in combat. If the airplane was pulled in tight and stalled at high speed at 2 "gs" or more with power on, turning right or left, the left wing would drop violently without warning and the airplane would flick onto its back from a left turn. I scored against a

190 under such circumstances. The message was clear, don't stall it. Our own Bell Aircobra P-39 would do the same thing.

Fighting Qualities. Excellent high speed, with exceptional maneuverability at those speeds. Range and endurance were markedly improved over the 109. The Focke Wulf would go 3 hours plus. Visibility with the full view canopy was superb, as it was in the Mustang.

Ju-88 and Me-110

The characteristics of both airplanes are given here in one comparative sketch because they comprise a class of airplanes that were never really successful; they were the twin engine fighters or "destroyers" that were, in this case at least, also supposed to be dive-bombers. We tried it here in this country too. There was an abortion called the YFM-1, more commonly known as the Bell "Airacuda"; a twin engine, Allison powered, pusher (rather than tractor) "destroyer." It had to be one of the doggiest flying machines ever built. The design gross weight was about 18,000 pounds and all-up flight weight was 21,600 pounds. It had a 5-man crew and the top speed was a rattling 268 mph at 13,000 feet. Maneuvers that were prohibited were the loop, roll, Immelman, inverted flight or spins. That about says it all.

General Chennault relates in his story how he argued himself hoarse for 5 days, as a member of the Pursuit Development Board at Wright Field, against the procurement of the airplane. He lost and the Army blew 2 million for 13 of them. Chennault climbed into his Boeing P-12 and went home literally half sick. Within a year he left the Army in disgust and frustration and was on his way to China as an advisor to Chiang Kai-shek to build an air force to confront the Japanese in China.

	JU-88A	ME-110
Mean weight, pounds	28,000 (4,000 lb. bombs)	13,800 (fighter)
Engines	Jumo 211J	DB-601A
Horsepower	1400 hp ea.	1150 hp. ea.
Power loading, lbs./hp	10.0	6.0
Wing loading, lbs./sq. ft.	51	33.3
Prop diameter, ft.	—	10.24
Wing geomerty		
Area, sq. ft.	549	415
Span, ft.	59.8	53.4
Mean chord, ft.	9.18	7.78
Dihedral, degrees	—	4.1 (outboard)
Sweepback, degrees	—	1.85
Root Chord, ft.	11.76	11.05
Tip Chord, ft.	4.56	4.6
Root Thickness	14.9	17.6
Tip Thickness	11.7	11.5
Aspect Ratio	6.5	6.86
Top speed, mph	290/15,000 ft.	340/22,000 ft.

Neither airplane was a match for any single fighter that the Allies had. They didn't have the speed or the small turning radius required. It's inappropriate to even refer to them as "fighters." By fighter standards the performance of either was bad.

Taken in the proper context of twin engine airplanes that had a minimum turning radius of about 1000 feet (Spit I or Hurricane I radius was 30% less) capable of doing light bomber or night fighter work against the RAF heavies they come out pretty well. The Me-110 lacked maneuverability at medium to high speeds; going from 200 mph to 400 mph the stick forces when from heavy to "solid." Surprisingly, the Ju-88 aileron control response was excellent at high speeds. At 300 mph, more than three quarters aileron could be applied with one hand. The corresponding roll rate definitely put it out of the bomber class in that respect and that was important in avoiding fighter attacks.

But the Ju-88 had some nasty habits as well as some interesting devices as flying aids. First, the airplane was not easy to land. It was very difficult to get the tail down, and the brakes were *particularly effective*. Compounding this feature was a tendency for the tail to swing after a wheel landing which must be corrected immediately. So while the tail is swinging you're dabbling with the brakes . . . and there you go, chasing yourself into a ground loop if your coordination is off.

Engine failure on takeoff, in a climb or under instrument conditions was a nasty experience in nearly every twin engine airplane of that era, theirs and ours. If you lost an engine under those conditions in a Ju-88 you were on the ragged edge of catastrophe. At 150 mph during a climb, even when prompt corrective action was taken to prevent the wing from dropping, over 1000 feet could be lost. If the flaps are set in the takeoff position during the climb, then the recovery was even more difficult, since the ailerons are heavier and the wing dropping maneuver is more violent. According to the British test crews, landing with one engine out was equally precarious due to the violent swing and bank caused by opening up the good engine to correct the final landing approach at low airspeeds.

The automatic dive bombing and pullout sequence was certainly innovative. Its purpose was to reduce pilot error and improve bombing accuracy. Any dive angle between 30 and 70 degrees could be used.

Before entering the dive a radio altimeter, which sounded a horn, was set for the selected height, at which the bombs were to be released. Bomb distribution was set by standard tables of data carried in the airplane. The elevator trim tab was set to a fixed mark, which trimmed the airplane nose heavy, and the the dive was started in the automatic mode. As the speed built up the dive brakes were extended and the engines throttled back. At the time the dive brakes came out the elevator trim tab moved up 2.5 degrees, causing the elevator to go down and the nose of the airplane to drop. This pitch down caused a brief uncomfortable negative "g" force. With that particular trim tab setting, the airplane would pitch over to about a 50 degree dive during which the speed reached about 310 mph after losing 6,000 feet. That isn't much speed but remember the brakes are out and the power is off.

During this time the pilot checks his dive angle by means of inclined lines painted on one of the cockpit window panels as they relate to the horizon. When the pre-set height was approached the radio altimeter set off the horn. On reaching the exact altitude the horn noise stops. At that instant the pilot pressed the release button.

On pressing the release button a spring loaded solenoid device pops the trim tab back 2.5 degree down. The elevator went up and the airplane pulled out at about 3.5 "gs."

In a full 70 degree dive from 8,000 feet, automatic pullout initiated at 2,000 feet, maximum speed reached was about 337 mph on a 3.5 "g" pullout. The minimum altitude at the bottom of the pullout was 300 feet. Rather sporty, I'd say; it would certainly liven up a dull afternoon.

In summary of the German aircraft, the Focke Wulf 190, and of course the ME-262, were by far the best fighters, and dazzling successes they were, too, in spite of their bad points. As I have related previously, given enough of them in a timely fashion, the Allied effort might have been in very serious trouble.

Allied Fighters

To keep the subject within reasonable limits, the discussion of the Allied fighters will be brief. I believe the reader is sufficiently familiar with them and that he will bear me no grudge for just hitting the "high spots", before we make a final evaluation.

There was an interesting fly-off between a P-47D and an FW-190A in England during the war years. Those data are credited to Master Sergeant Merle Olmstead, one of the crew chiefs in my squadron during those years and also a writer and collector of aviation flora and fauna. For clarity and brevity, it is presented in report form.

Aircraft employed. A P-47D-4 with a combat load of fuel and ammo and an FW-190A with two loaded cannon and two loaded 7.6mm machine guns. The P-47 had water injection and the FW-190 was in exceptionally good condition, pulling 42 inches on the manifold at takeoff, which was its all-up power rating.

Pilots. The pilot of the P-47 had about 200 hours in a P-40, with 17 months of combat experience. The pilot of the Fw-190 had 300 hours in twin engine aircraft and 500 hours in single engine stuff, but no combat experience. Each pilot had 5 hours in their test airplanes, thus their experience was about even.

Test Program. Four separate flights of one hour each were conducted. All speeds are indicated air speeds.

Recorded Results

1. Acceleration from 200 mph to full power at 5,000 ft. The Fw-190 accelerated faster than the P-47 initially and gained 200 yards, but at 330 mph the P-47 rapidly overtook the 190 and gained about 2,000 yards very quickly and was still accelerating. Water injection was used on the P-47. (Note: The P-47 was 5,000 pounds heavier).

2. Climb **2,000 feet to 8,500 feet**. Starting at 250 mph both airplanes were pulled up sharply to the maximum angle of climb. The Fw-190 passed the P-47 through the first 1500 feet but the T-bolt overtook it and steadily out-climbed it by 500 feet per minute. The P-47 used water injection and overheated slightly, the Fw-190 did not overheat. **10,000 feet to 15,000 feet**. Starting at 250 mph the 190 again outclimbed the P-47 through the first 1,000 feet but the P-47 overtook the 190 and reached 15,000 feet ahead of it.

3. Diving from 10,000 feet to 3,000 feet. Starting from 250 mph, diving at an angle of 65 degrees with constant throttle setting, the 190 pulled away at the beginning but the P-47 passed it at 3,000 feet at a much higher speed and had a much better pull out.

4. Turning at 10,000 feet in excess of 250 mph. The P-47 easily out turned the 190 and had to throttle back to keep from overruning it. The superiority of the P-47 in turning increased with altitude. Below 250 mph the 190 was able to bang on its propeller more and turn inside the P-47 in flat turns. The P-47 was able, however, by doing maximum climbs and dives while pulling around in the tightest turns, to end up on the 190's tail. The P-47 built up more speed in the dives and hence climbed higher and faster. The P-47 pilot then waited for the 190 to reach its stall point below him

and when it fell away, he'd kick the T-bolt over and be in firing position.

On balance the reader should remember that, as I said in the beginning, *Whichever Pilot saw the other one first had the winnning advantage*. Small differences in a single characteristic didn't matter much. It was the total capability of the airplane and the pilot that counted.

I would like to make special mention of another feature that is not a performance characteristic but it had everything to do with survival, that is **Structural Integrity**, the ability to sustain combat damage and still stay airborne. The P-47 and the B-17 will live forever in the drama of combat aviation by virtue of the damage they could sustain. You couldn't get the public to believe some of the stories unless you had the photos to prove it, of which there are an abundance. Without that evidence they'd shake their heads and lead you off to the Funny Farm. The designers deserve a salute. The "Fort" and the "Jug" were not equaled by any other airplanes that I know of in this respect.

—Kit Carson

Chapter 10
Requiem For An Air Force

There was a great deal of grousing at Leiston Airbase, on the east coast of England, that late spring of 1945 when word reached the "Yoxford Boys" of the 357th Fighter Group, that they were to be part of the occupation forces which would soon take up station in a defeated Germany.

The 357th was not one of the better known units of the old 8th Air Force, yet it had compiled a remarkable record in 14 months of combat. With 609½ air-to-air victory claims, it ranked higher than the famous 4th Fighter Group, which had been in combat more than twice as long, and was surpassed in air-to-air victories only by the veteran 56th Fighter Group. The 357th had other distinctions—it was the first group in the 8th Air Force to fly the superb Merlin Mustang, and it had, on the 14th of January, 1945, destroyed more enemy aircraft in one engagement than any other comparable sized unit in history. On that date 56 Luftwaffe fighters were shot down in a wild melee over the Berlin area, for the loss of only three Mustangs.

The Group had been christened "Yoxford Boys" by "Lord Haw Haw", a British turncoat who regularly broadcast Nazi propaganda over various German radio stations. His sources of information were suspect however, as the 357th's base was a considerable distance from the village of Yoxford, and much closer to the town of Leiston. Nevertheless, the Group was proud of its Nazi supplied nickname, and its detractors had little cause for gloating. With the end of the war in Europe however, all of the events were nothing but material for future history books.

It had been widely thought, in that spring of 1945, that units leaving the 8th Air Force would probably head for the Pacific to join the war against Japan, and most of the troops thought the brief period at home before deploying to the Pacific, would make it worth it, but the occupation force announcement changed all that.

Neubiberg Airbase (Allied code R-85), near Munich became the new home of the 357th Fighter Group, which had arrived there during June and July. It had been a long and hectic journey for part of the Group, which had brought the unit's vehicles and heavy equipment overland across a battered Europe, but for the air echelon, it had been an easy B-17 ride. Duty at R-85 was not difficult, and there was considerable free time. Quarters were positively plush compared to those left in England. The war had apparently had little effect on German breweries in the Munich area, and squadron beer parties on the tree lined lawns were frequent and noisy.

Off base freedom, however, was tight in the early days of the occupation and "no fraternization" was the cardinal rule. Nevertheless, there were numerous group tours in the inevitable 2½ ton truck, to heavily bombed Munich, to the ghastly concentration camp at Dachau, and into the beautiful Alps of Southern Germany.

Weapons Found

Unlimited supplies of German weapons were available for the taking, and target shooting and hunting were popular forms of recreation. Ammunition could be found in numerous ammunition dumps in the vicinity, and thousands of rounds of 7.92 mm machine gun ammunition were discovered in the attic of the 362nd Fighter Squadron's hangar. We broke the belts down and fired most of it—ball, tracer, etc., through the many Mauser rifles which were available. Sporterizing these rifles was another popular hobby and these could be legally shipped home by parcel post.

For the aviation enthusiast, occupied Germany was a never ending wonderland. When the author arrived at Neubiberg, via B-17, in June or July, there were about 60 Me 109s and Fw 190s lined up in a far corner of the field. More were in an unfinished hangar which had been under construction among the trees at the edge of the flying field. Although some of the aircraft had minor damage, most were in good shape, and some still had "hot" guns. One of these 109s was towed to the maintenance hangars and work begin to bring it to an airworthy state. Most of the American pilots were eager to fly the captured equipment, but only a few had the opportunity. Before the 357th Messerschmitt was ready to fly, a pilot at another base was killed while flying an Fw 190, and orders soon arrived forbidding the flying of any enemy equipment (Fig. 10-1).

Across the field from the parked 109s and 190s, and near the hangar line, was a large aircraft dump, containing dozens of

Fig. 10-1. At war's end, countless Luftwaffe aircraft were found intact, unable to fly due to lack of fuel or even tires—mute evidence of the effectiveness of the US strategic bombing effort against key German industries.

Luftwaffe airplanes in various states of damage, from near flyable to total wrecks. Memories of so many flying years ago are not clear enough to identify all types in the dump, but it contained most of the common types, and photos taken at the time show a Me 109 with what appear to be Hungarian markings, while Me 262s, Ju 87s and 88s, Fw 190s, Me 110s, and He 111s and a few Fw 44 trainers are remembered. In addition to these aircraft, there was a vast assortment of engines, gun packs, maintenance equipment and parts. Near the dump, but not in it, a Fw 190 rested on its belly and from a Me 109 in this dump came a control stick head which still graces the author's desk, in the form of a lamp.

Completing the assortment of enemy aircraft, was a Siebel 204, a Me 109, and a 190 (with a flat tire), all parked on the hangar line.

As American units were deactivated in Europe, their aircraft began to arrive at Neubiberg in large numbers and in an amazing array which belied the title of Fighter Group. Almost all types used in the late European war made their way into the hands of the 357th Group, most of them on their way to the scrapyards. Perhaps the most useful were the lowly Taylor L-4s and Stinson L-5s. These were "fun" airplanes and it wasn't long before a few of the pilots found themselves drafted as flight instructors, with a waiting list of mechanics eager to try their hand. In the author's squadron it didn't last long though, the L-4 on hand at that time was washed out when its crew buzzed a man on a bicycle and misjudged the pullout . . . into some nearby tree. There were no casualties, but the L-4 was totaled.

There were other strange birds on Neubiberg's ramps in that long ago summer. The big Dornier 335s (there were two of them) are remembered for their excessive noise, a good turn of speed, and an inability to accomplish much in a friendly dog-fight with a P-51.

Both of the Dorniers had arrived by air—the only flyable German aircraft seen that summer. The two seat machine had come in first, with a German civilian test pilot at the controls. Unable to resist the temptation to show off his airplane, he had thundered down across the hangar line in a classic buzz job. The buzz job, a common, but often deadly spectacle, was one of the phenomena of WW II, now all but extinct because of heavy penalties against any military pilot foolish enough to do it.

Later on, the single seater version was flown into Neubiberg, and still later both departed for unknown destinations, the single seater being turned over to the RAF.

A Russian was there too. Totally lost, he landed his Yak 9 on Neubiberg's steel matt runway and stayed several weeks awaiting the necessary departure clearance from "above". Our 150 grade fuel was too rich for the Yak's engine and it was refueled with gasoline drained from German aircraft. The Russian finally flew happily away into the sunset with one main gear leg still down. One wonders what his fate was after fraternizing with the Americans.

Aircraft Wreckage

The wreckage of thousands of aircraft lay scattered across the landscape of Germany, and one warm Sunday this writer and a companion hiked along the *autobahn* towards Salzburg to see what else could be found of interest. Only a short distance from the airbase we spotted the wing of an Me 109 lodged high in treetops just off the road—no sign of the rest of the wreck—just a wing.

Further down the road, in a large forest clearing, were dozens of German aircraft, mostly bombers and transports. How they got there is a mystery, possibly it was a collection point for damaged aircraft, as all of them were. These aircraft were not on an airfield, however, and there was no sign of any facilities.

Many German airfields had become untenable in the last months of the war, due to the close attention given them by large roving bands of Allied fighters, which literally ruled the skies of Germany. Because of this, the Luftwaffe used many straight stretches of *autobahn* as runways, hiding the aircraft under the trees when not flying. The wreckage of these airplanes were common along the roads after the war, and it is possible that the bombers referred to above had used the nearby *autobahn* for their last landing.

It had, all in all, been a relaxed and interesting summer, but for most of the troops the dominant question was still "when do we go home?" A few who had no ties at home stayed on. Most units were offering instant promotions to entice men to remain in service, but the flow of personnel back to the Zone of Interior soon became a flood, and combat organizations, such as the 357th at Neubiberg, were combat units in name only.

By October, the rush of men returning to the U.S. had so drained the 357th Fighter Grp. of mechanics and other maintenance personnel, that only about ten P-51s could be kept operational.

It was in October that the summer of '45 ended for this writer, but one more airfield was to be examined. A week was spent at Augsburg awaiting transport to France. This field also had a huge dump full of shattered and broken aircraft, but a two seat Fw 190 and a similar Me 109 were both in flyable condition when I last saw them. The two seat 190 was without markings, and by a stroke of luck I later heard from an ex-Luftwaffe pilot, who had planned to escape a crumbling German in this same aircraft. The plans had gone awry, by my correspondent had survived. His companion in the scheme had not.

The transport provided for our ride to the French ports turned out to be the familiar "40 & 8" freight cars of WWI fame. (We envied some of our traveling companions who were assigned passenger cars until we discovered they had no seats, the window glass was gone from all of them, and they were full of bullet holes—a final testimony to the power of Allied tactical air in the late war.)

—*Merle C. Olmstead*

Index